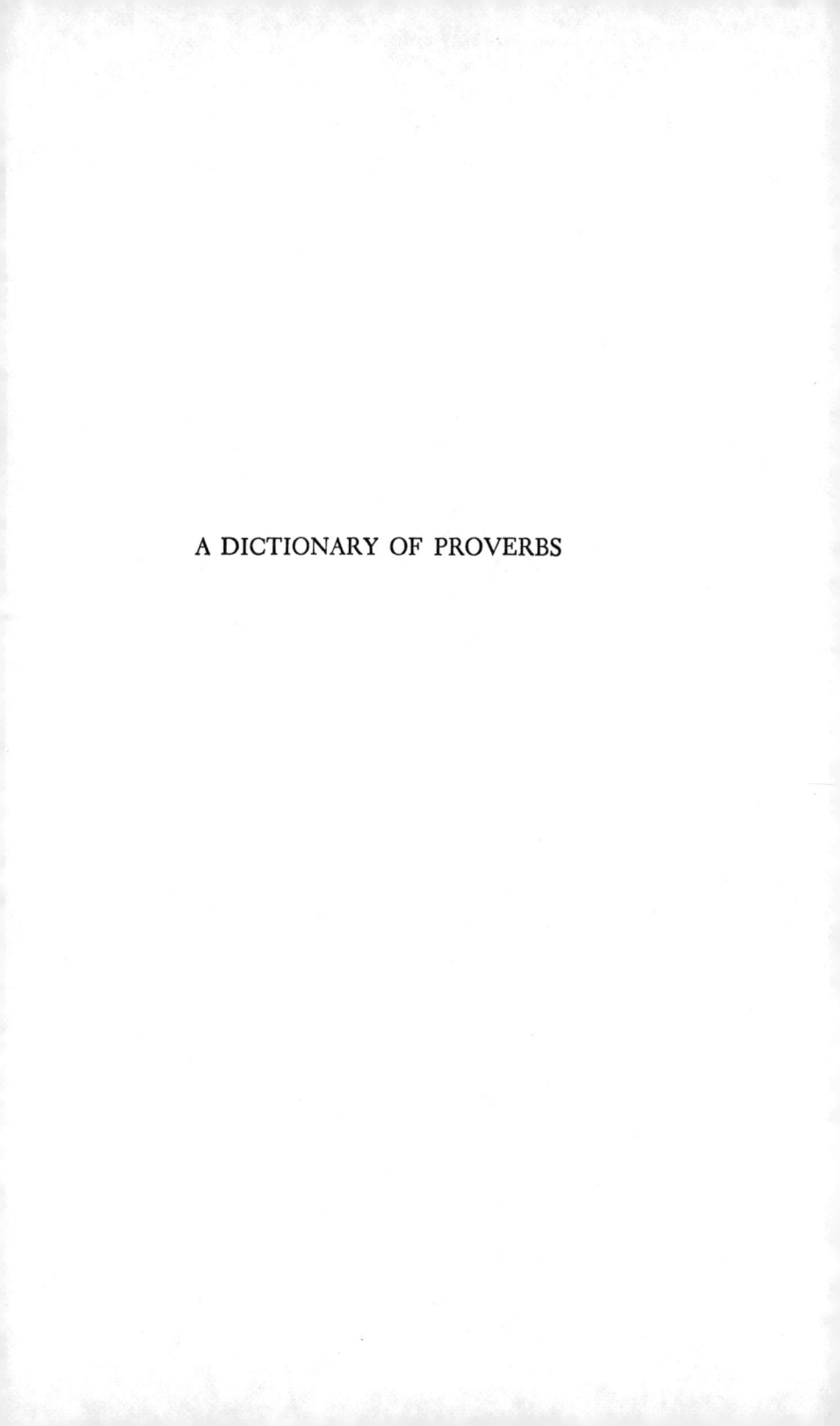

A DICTIONARY OF PROVERBS

A DICTIONARY OF PROVERBS

With a Collection of Maxims, Phrases, Passages, Poems and Anecdotes from Ancient and Modern Literature

By

PETROS D. BAZ, M.D.

By the same author
"Gems of Wisdom"
"The Parents of Man's Fortune"

A Philosophical Paperback

Philosophical Library
New York

Copyright, 1963, by Philosophical Library, Inc.
200 West 57th Street, New York, N.Y. 10019.
All rights reserved.
Manufactured in the United States of America.

ISBN 8022-0086-9
LC Cat. #62-21555

DEDICATED TO M. N.

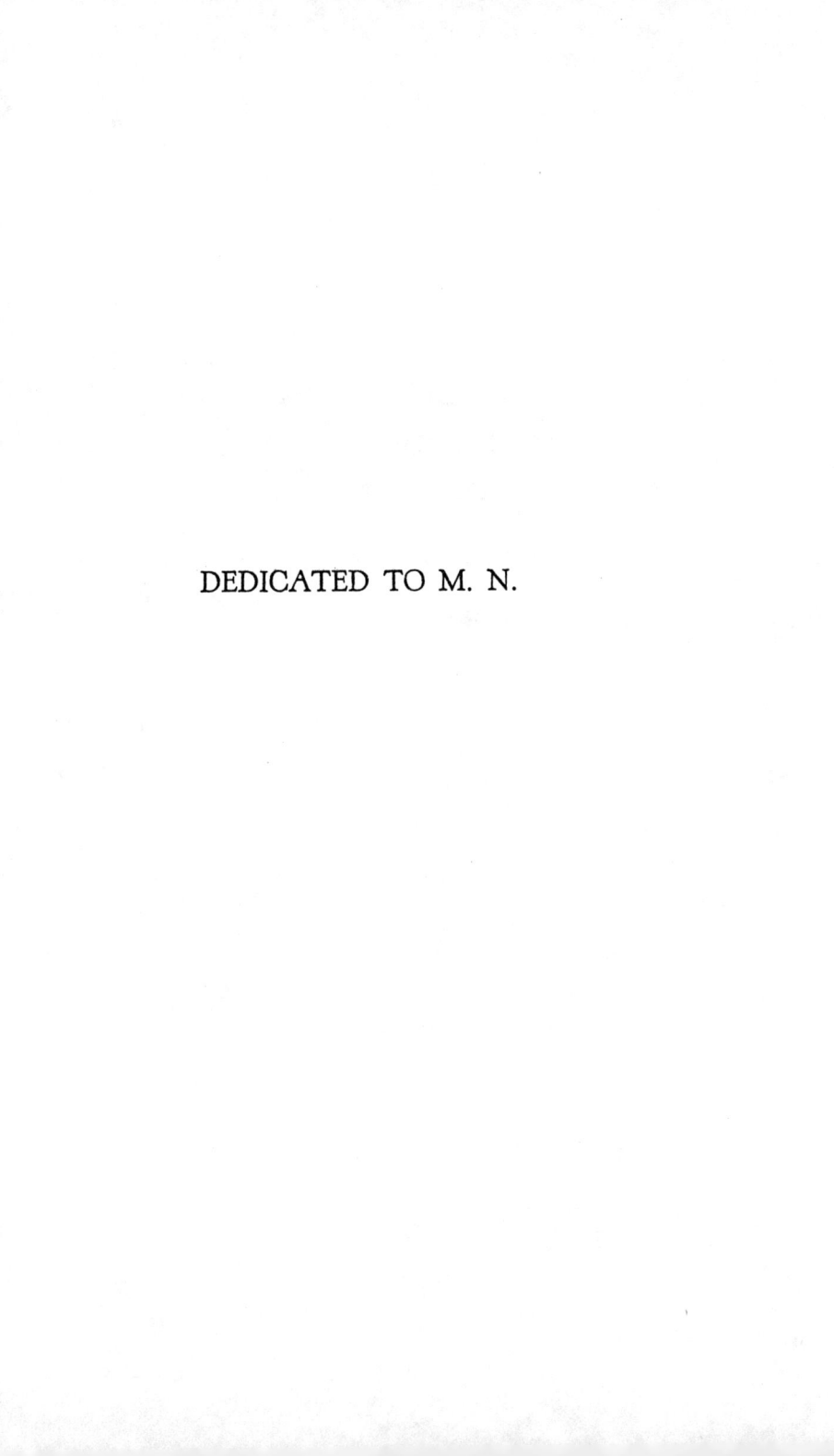

> GET WISDOM
> GET UNDERSTANDING
> FORGET IT NOT!

"Either write things worth reading or do things worth writing."
—(Franklin)

CONTENTS

Introduction xi

PART ONE

Maxims, Phrases, Passages, Poems and Anecdotes from Ancient and Modern Literature 1

PART TWO

A Dictionary of Proverbs 17

PART THREE

Selected Quotations 153

The path of the just is as the shining light that shineth more and more unto the perfect day.

Proverbs 4:18

"Eyes Have They, and See Not"

"Hide not your light under a basket."

Dear Reader,

As a famous writer lay dying he was heard to murmur the words—"More light! More light!" Men and women need not only light for their bodies, but also they need light for their minds and souls. For many of them as St. Chrysostom (A.D. 40-120) said, "are like those who suffer from sore eyes, they find the light painful: while the darkness which permits them to see nothing is restful and agreeable." "Walk while ye have the light, lest darkness come upon you."

As a piece of unwonted luxury Epictetus, the Stoic philosopher who lived in the first century, had purchased a little iron lamp. It was the only possession which he had and a thief stole it. "He will be finely disappointed when he comes again," quietly observed Epictetus, "for he will only find an earthenware lamp next time." At his death the little earthenware lamp was bought by some genuine hero-worshipper for 3,000 drachma. "The purchaser hoped," says the satirical Lucian, "that if he read philosophy at night by that lamp, he would at once acquire in dreams the wisdom of the admirable old man who purchased it."

"To the poet, to the philosopher, to the saint, all things are friendly and sacred, all events profitable, all days holy, all men divine." —Morrison.

In obedience to the order of the Council of Constance (1415), the remains of John Wycliffe (1324-1384), one of the most eminent ecclesiastics of his time who adopted the principles of Reformation and translated the Bible into English, were exhumed and burned to ashes, there cast into the Swift, a neighboring brook running hard by; and "then this brook hath conveyed his ashes into Avon, Avon into Severn, Severn into the narrow Seas, they into the main ocean. And thus the ashes of Wycliffe are the emblems of his doctrine which is now dispersed all the world over."

What the compass and instruments are to the navigational officer and the ordnance map is to the field officer so this book is to you. It will give light to your mind and soul in your journey through life. This is the emblem of our doctrine and let us disperse it all the world over.

THE AUTHOR

Introduction

"Wisdom is to the soul what health is to the body."

There is a story of a young man who came to the famous Greek scholar, Socrates, asking, "What shall I do to become a learned man?" Whereupon Socrates led him to a pool of water, plunged the young man's head under and held it there. When the youth had struggled free and got his breath, Socrates asked, "When your head was under the water, what did you most wish?" "Air," gasped the young man. "Very well," answered the Sage, "When you want knowledge as much as you wanted air when your head was under the water, you will find ways to get it." Here is counsel from a man who was willing to learn. "A wise man is strong: Yea, a man of knowledge increaseth strength." *Proverbs XXIV.* "As new born babies desire the sincere milk of the word that you may grow thereby." "Let fame be the thirst of youth." John Ruskin (1819-1901) mentions that at the gate of that silent Faubourg, St. Germain, there is but brief questions, "Do you desire to enter? Pass! Do you ask to be the companion of nobles? Make yourself noble, and you shall be. Do you long for the conversation of the wise? Learn to understand it, and you shall hear it. But on other terms? No. If you will rise to us, we cannot stoop to you."

"Men do not care how nobly they live, but only how long, although, it is within the reach of every man to live nobly, but within no man's power to live long."—Seneca (8 B.C.-65 A.D.). "The world is purified not by action, but nobleness of life. Therefore, be noble and the nobleness that lies in other men, sleeping but never dead will rise in majesty to meet thine own."—*Lowell.* "We can finish nothing in this life but we may make a beginning, and bequeath a noble example."—*Smiler.* "Nobilitas sola est atque unica virtus." (Nobility is the one only virtue)—*Juvenal.* Seneca also said, "Live among men as if God beheld you; speak to God as if men were listening."

"A short period of life is long enough for living well and honorably."—*Cicero* (106-43 B.C.). Herodotus (485-424 B.C.) said: "Nothing in human life is more to be lamented than that a wise man should have so little influence." Nothing will be more lamented than that some may read the following pages and still keep themselves in darkness and not apply these truths to life. "Apply thine heart unto instruction, and thine ear to the words of knowledge."—*Proverbs* 23:12.

From ancient times, learned men and women, philosophers from the East have adopted wise sayings and parables as the easiest medium of conveying their dignified teachings to all classes of people. But unfortunately in later years, this lofty custom is disappearing and falling into darkness. "He has half the deed done who has made a beginning."—*Horace*. "For a web begun, God sends thread." "There is not some moment without some duty." (Cicero). As Diogenes of ancient Greece is reported to have gone about day and night carrying a lantern and looking for an honest man, so I have for many years collected one by one these quotations and maxims from several languages. I have carefully compiled them in this dictionary which is a guide to all people and contains profound lessons of moral wisdom which is food for everybody's soul. This book is like a telescope: If a man looks through the telescope, he sees the world beyond; if he looks at the telescope he sees nothing but it. Or it is like a rich Persian carpet. The beautiful figures and patterns of which can be shown only by spreading and extending it out. When it is contracted and folded up, they are obscure and lost. I want this wisdom, loyalty and efficiency to characterize the attitude and acts of every reader.

"The lasting monuments are paper monuments." Edward de Bury said, "The glory of the world would be buried in oblivion had not God as a remedy conferred on man the benefit of books." "A man is himself plus the books he reads." But books, which I call my silent friends, must be good. For, as Milton says, a good book "is a precious life blood of a master spirit." Charles Dickens (1812-1870) said, "There are books of which the backs and covers are by far the best parts." Helen Keller (1880-   ) who was blind and deaf since infancy said, "Literature is my Utopia. Here I am not disfranchised. No barrier of the scenes shuts me out from the sweat, gracious embarrassment, or awkwardness." "The books which help one most are those which make one think the most." "Books are the legacies that a great genius leaves to mankind which are delivered down from generation to generation, as presents to the posterity of those who are yet unborn."—*Addison*. It is my desire that each sentence in this book will make you think. "Books are for wisdom, piety, diligence or use."—*Denham*. There was

an inscription for the children's reading room, Hopkinton, Mass., which read:
> "Books are keys to wisdom's treasure:
> Books are gates to lands of pleasure:
> Books are paths that upward lead:
> Books are friends, come, let us read."

This is a book of wisdom; read it, digest it, and keep it in your home or library. "For a home without books is like a body without a soul." Erasmus wrote to Bishop Fisher (1524), "I know how busy you are in your library, which is your Paradise." An ancient inscription over the door of the library at Thebes reads: "Medicine for the Soul." Francis Bacon said (1561-1626) "Reading maketh a full man; conference a ready man; and writing an exact man." He also said, "Some books are to be tasted; others to be swallowed; and some few to be chewed and digested." Life is too short to read inferior books. Charles Lamb (1775-1834) said "Books think for me." Starrett said, "Westminster Abbey is a Mausoleum; the book borrowers in Charing Cross Road are resurrection grounds."

It is said that the author who speaks about his own book is almost as bad as a mother who talks about her own children. But we feel that here is a book which will be indispensable for every public and school library; for every clergyman, public speaker and lawyer; for every editorial writer and every writer in historical or literary subjects; for every teacher and every student.

It is not only a dictionary of proverbs but it contains also many interesting quotations included at the end of this book. "Whose lines are mottoes of the heart, whose truths electrify the sage"—*Campbell.*

Therefore,
> "Let this book be your study and delight,
> Read it by day and meditate upon it by night."

"Be not like the fisherman whose feet are in the water but his face unwashed."

> Wisdom to the foolish is diamond set in lead,
> By their own paltry notions through the vale of life are led.
> But wisdom's truth is to the wise,
> A faithful guide that never dies.
> This book though only small in size,
> Is wealth, in it much truth there lies.
> Thus have I written sound advice

For all men know that good advice
Is far beyond the greatest price.
As there are people who are wise,
So there are others who are otherwise.
If you would have the wise man's mind,
Then read this book, if you don't mind,
And if to friends you would be kind,
Commend this book, for of its kind
There's only one you as will find.
Peruse then, Friend, my little book,
For with it wish I you good luck.

Most of the proverbs mentioned here have been made and due credit not given. This is because their sources have long since been forgotten and only the burning, convicting message of them remains. Some of the famous authors are mentioned here:

1. *Homer*—850 BC—the most famous Greek of all epic poets; author of the "Iliad and the Odyssey."
2. *Socrates*—(469-399 BC)—the distinguished Greek philosopher who devoted himself to study and began to exhort the people on public questions and the conduct of life.
3. *Plato*—(429-347 BC)—the renowned Greek philosopher. His writings are among the greatest works of the ancients and are admired in all succeeding ages. He was a prizewinning athlete, a brave soldier, a poet. He invented day nurseries, kindergarten methods, etc.
4. *Aristotle*—(384-322 BC)—disciple of Plato and teacher of Alexander the Great: founder of the School of Philosophy in Athens.
5. *Horace (Horatius)*—(65 BC-8 AD)—the famous Roman satirist.
6. *Ovid*—(43 BC-18 AD)—the famous Roman philosopher.
7. *Epictetus*, the Stoic philosopher, who lived in the First Century and was a moral teacher of great repute and influence. He was a slave and was honored by the Emperor Hadrian himself.
8. *Seneca*—(4 BC-65 AD)—the famous Roman philosopher.
9. *Mar Aprem*—(303-373 AD)
   Mar Narsai—(434-502 AD)—the famous poets and philosophers in the Aramaic or Syriac language.
10. *Omar Khayyam (Died 1123 AD)*—great Persian poet.
11. *Mutanaby (916-966 AD)*—and *Abu-Alla Muarry (blind)*—(973-1058 AD)—the famous Arab philosophers.
12. *Dante (1265-1321 AD)*—the greatest of Italian poets. He was the torch bearer of the Renaissance. His "Divine Comedy" was the first work written in the Italian vernacular.

13. *Erasmus* (1466-1545 AD)—the great Dutch philosopher who wrote "Adagia of Erasmus," containing some four thousand Greek and Roman proverbs.
14. *Montaigne* (1533-1592 AD)—a French essayist of world-wide fame.
15. *Cervantes* (1547-1616 AD)—world famous Spanish author who died in poverty.
16. *Voltaire* (1694-1778 AD)—one of the greatest French philosophers and writers.
17. *La Rouchefoucauld* (1613-1680 AD)—a renowned French statesman and writer of the Louis XIV period. His reflections and moral maxims are classic.
18. *La Fontaine* (1621-1695 AD)—the celebrated French poet and writer of fables.
19. *Milton* (1608-1695 AD)—England's chief epic poet whose "Paradise Lost" is the greatest poem of its kind.
20. *Shakespeare* (1564-1616 AD)—England's greatest poet and dramatist.
21. *Franklin* (1706-1790 AD)—American statesman and philosopher. Writer of "Poor Richard's Almanac," a book of wise and witty sayings. The man who captured lightning.
22. *Tolstoy* (1828-1910 AD)—most distinguished personality of modern Russian literature.

In conclusion, I wish to thank Rev. W. O. Hern for his helpful suggestions. I also wish to acknowledge the unfailing courtesy and efficiency of the publisher and printers.

PETROS D. BAZ, M.D.

Part I

"Woe to Them That Are Wise in Their Own Eyes"

What is a proverb? Bacon calls it, "An edged tool of speech." Lord Russell defines it as "The wisdom of many and the wit of one." But according to Rayner, "It is a salty sentence which precipitates some nebulous truth into people's minds."

Learning is the eye of the mind, but many perish in the earth through vain learning. "A learned man is like a well-cut stone." "A single day among the learned lasts longer than the longest life of the ignorant." (Seneca). "Man's best candle is his understanding." "No one is born learned, but learning without understanding is useless." Or as Goethe said, "What we do not understand, we do not possess." Plato said, "Bodily exercise, when compulsory, does no harm to the body; but knowledge which is acquitted under compulsion obtains no hold on the mind." A Chinese proverb says, "Learning without thought is dangerous." An old Arab proverb says, "The ink of the learned is as precious as the blood of the martyr." "For one drop of ink may make millions think."

The wisest man is he who does not think he is, or as Socrates puts it, "That man is wisest who realizes that his wisdom is worthless." Sir Isaac Newton (1642-1727 AD) said to one who praised his wisdom, "I am a child on the seaside picking up a pebble here and a shell there, but the great ocean of truth still lies before me." Thomas Edison (1847-1931) who patented over 1300 inventions once said, "I do not know one millionth part of one percent about anything." Michelangelo (1475-1564) the world's most famous painter, sculptor and architect, once said, "Ancora Imparo"—still I am learning. We can say, "Ancora impariamo"—still we are learning. When the great astronomer, Kepler, gazed into the skies, through the giant telescope, he said, "O, God, I am thinking thy thoughts after thee."

Years ago a young officer of the British Navy discovered a small dangerous rock in the Mediterranean Sea and reported it to the admiralty. All stations were immediately notified to mark the spot on the charts. An old captain was the first to sail that way and he said, "There is no such a rock. I've sailed this sea all my life, and I know."

Thereupon, he ordered the ship to sail right over the spot under full sail. There followed a mighty crash and the broken vessel with all hands went down. The captain knew too much and refused to follow the charts of the sea. "Pride goeth before destruction and an haughty spirit before a fall." Samuel Pepys (1633-1703) said, "I pray God to keep me from being proud." "Some take pride in their looks, others in their race, others in their business, others in their social life. In other words, pride may be spiritual, intellectual, material or social." —Billy Graham. When Viscount de Turenne who was Marshal of France in the time of Louis XIV gained a battle, he always wrote in his dispatches: "We succeeded" so as to give the credit to the rest of the army; but if he was defeated, he wrote: "I lost," so as to take all the blame upon himself.

Solomon, who was "wiser than all men" and who studied plant life, bird life, insect life and wrote three thousand proverbs, said: "Seest thou a man wise in his own conceit? There is more hope of a fool than of him." (Proverbs 26:12). Conceit, envy, jealousy ("the jaundice of the soul"—Dryden), and pride of opinion keep the mind hide-bound and play a man's life into the hands of that great enemy prejudice. Antisthones used to say that "Envious people were devoured by their own disposition, just as iron is by rust." Pope Gregory the Great (540-604) divided all sins under seven heads. They are called "the seven deadly sins." They are: "Pride, anger, envy, impurity, gluttony, slothfulness (laziness, idleness) and avarice."

There is a Greek story about a man who killed himself, through envy. His fellow citizens had erected a statue to one of their number who was a celebrated champion in the public games. But this man, a rival of the honored athlete, was so envious that he vowed that he would destroy the statue. Every night he went out into the darkness and chiselled at its base in an effort to undermine its foundation and make it fall. At last he succeeded. It did fall—but it fell on him. He fell a victim of his own envy. "Tell me," said the willow to the thorn, "why art thou so envious of the clothes of those who pass by? Of what use can they be to thee?" "None whatsoever," replied the thorn. "I have no desire to wear them—I only want to tear them." "The envious man grows thin at another man's prosperity."—Horace. "Envy is a pain of mind that successful men cause their neighbors." (Orrasander).

About pride, it is said that once the philosopher Plato entertained some friends in a room where there was a richly ornamented couch. One of his friends came in, very dirty as usual, and getting on the couch and trampling on it, said, "I trample upon the pride of Plato." Plato answered, mildly, "But with greater pride, my friend." Seneca said, "Let him who hath conferred a favour hold his tongue."

In conferring a favor nothing should be more avoided than pride. Pride, ambition, lust, avarice, etc., are nothing but species of madness although not mentioned among the diseases in our medical books. Pride is therefore, "Pleasure arriving from a man's thinking too highly of himself." Alexander wept when he heard from Anaxarchus that there was an infinite number of worlds; and his friends asked him if any accident had befallen him. He returned this answer, "Do you not think it a matter worthy of lamentation that when there is such a vast multitude of them, we have not yet conquered one?" "But among all the diseases of the mind, there is not one more epidemic or more pernicious than the love of flattery. (Steele).

"'Tis an old maxim in the schools
That flattery's the food of fools." (Swift)

Memory is the diary that we all carry about with us. (Oscar Wilde). It is also called the wonder of the brain, or as Shakespeare put it, "The warden of the brain." It is the treasurer and the guardian of all things. Charles Dickens prayed, "Lord, keep my memory green." Cyrus, King of Persia, who conquered Babylon in 538 and died in 528 BC, knew by heart the name of every soldier in his army. America's first famous poet, William C. Bryant (1794-1878), had a remarkable memory. He knew the alphabet before he was two. While on an ocean trip, he was too sick to read. He would spend hours reciting page after page of poetry from memory. He was the editor of the *New York Evening Post* for 52 years.

Many a man, however, fails to be a thinker for the sole reason that his memory is too good. "He that will eat the kernel of the nut must break the shell." Therefore, not only memorize, but think over all these wise sayings which you will need every day in your life, as there is no proverb which is not true.

"What sculpture is to a block of marble, so education is to the soul." Maxwell counts twelve points in character education:

1. Care of health
2. Correcting bad habits
3. Courage
4. Courtesy
5. Diligence
6. Forgiveness
7. Gratitude
8. Helpfulness
9. Honesty
10. Kindness
11. Obedience
12. Patience

Permit me to write about the first two items only. Without health, no one can fully fulfill his obligations to himself, to his fellow beings, or to his Creator. An Arabic proverb says, "Health is a crown on a well man's head, but no one can see it but a sick man." Thomas Carlyle (1794-1881) said, "Ill health of body or of mind is defeat. . . . Health alone is victory. Let all men, if they can manage it continue to be healthy." He also said, "Blessed is the healthy nature. It is coherent, sweetly cooperative not incoherent, self-distracting, self-destructive one." Walton said, "Health is the second blessing that we mortals are capable of—a blessing that money cannot buy." For maintaining health, here are my ABC's of health:

A. At night open the windows well.
B. Breathe deeply in the morning till you make your chest swell.
C. Chill and draught avoid, and take daily exercise.
D. Dwelling in damp houses is unwise.
E. Eat regularly, slowly and chew thoroughly well.
F. Flies, mosquitoes and dirt are enemies in the house in which you dwell.
G. Give first attention to fresh air and sunshine.
H. Having vegetables and fruits to eat daily is healthful and fine.
I. Illness many times comes from carelessness.
J. Just avoid overeating, smoking, and drinking which causes suffering and distress.
K. Keep always your clothes and skin clean.
L. Look carefully that no dust in the corners is seen.
M. Make a habit of keeping your bowels moving regularly.
N. Never accustom yourself to purges frequently.
O. Old and young people need special care.
P. Providing them with meat and hard food is not fair.
Q. Quietness and rest are needed much by them as well as fresh air.
R. Right is the motto and let us make it our goal.
S. "Sacred thy body even as thy soul."
T. Think well your health is better than wealth many times.
U. Use therefore your brains to remember my rhymes.
V. Valuable lives can be saved by asking early medical advice.
W. Wisdom has been given us: how to use it we have to realize.
X. X-rays and laboratories for the diagnosis are useful advice.
Y. You and I should be cheerful and work while we work and sleep while we sleep.
Z. Zero is our life and nil our qualities unless always good health we keep.

Therefore, try to be healthy and cheerful all the while.
Cross life's darkness with a smile.
If a man does not take care of his own health, he is doing himself a great harm and guilt.
Let us make it our motto and remember every day
That we need a "Healthy mind in a healthy body."
"There's no joy even in beautiful wisdom, unless one has holy health."
—(Ceos).

For correcting bad habits here is a true story: two brothers were convicted of stealing sheep in the olden days in England. In accordance with the brutal punishment of those days, they were branded in the forehead with the letters ST—Sheep Thief. One brother, unable to bear the stigma fled to a foreign country, where he tried to hide himself. He wandered from land to land, and at last died full of bitterness, and was buried in a forgotten grave. The other brother repented of his misdeed and did not try to run away from home. He said, "I can't get away from the fact that I once stole sheep, but I will remain here until I win back the respect of my neighbors and my own self-respect." The years passed and he gradually established a reputation for respectability and integrity, honesty and worth. At last a stranger in town saw an old man hobbling along with the letters ST branded on his forehead and asked a native what the letters signified. After thinking a while, the villager said, "It all happened a long time ago, and I have forgotten the particulars, but I think the letters are an abbreviation for Saint."

> "Whene'er a noble deed is wrought,
> Whene'er is spoken a noble thought,
> Our hearts, in glad surprise
> To higher levels rise." (Longfellow)

"No evil can happen to a good man either in life or after death." (Socrates). "If we are going to let our lights shine simply to illumine our own faces, we might as well let them go out." (Gordon).

Speaking further about education, Joseph Addison said, "I consider a human soul without education like marble in a quarry, which shows none of its inherent beauties till the skill of the polisher fetches out the colors, makes the surface shine, and discovers every ornamental spot and vein that runs through the body of it." But education, as Melville said, "Should be as gradual as the moonrise, perceptible not in progress but in result." "He who plants a tree does well; he who fells and saws it into planks does well; he who makes a bench of the planks does well: he who sitting on a bench teaches a child, does better than the rest." (*Dean Farrar*).

On one occasion, Aristotle was asked how much educated men were superior to those uneducated. "As much," said he, "as the living are to the dead." I would like to write the following two stories as instance of the benefit of education and vice versa.

It is said that some years ago in Persia, a merchant died leaving two wives each the mother of a son. One of the wives was educated while the other was not. After a short time, the son of the ignorant widow lost all that he had inherited from his father whereas the son of the learned lady obtained possession of all his father's inheritance in addition to several other things. He supported his poor brother with his mother, giving them the necessities of life.

One day a relative of the poor youth visited him and asked for reason of his poverty and his brother's incredible wealth; for both had received the same amount of property from the inheritance of their father. The poor unfortunate youth sighed and said: "My brother was influenced by his mother and I was influenced by mine. On account of kindness to me, my mother always hindered me from work and persuaded me to go to the garden and enjoy myself or to rest at home and so I had to live without earning my income. My brother's mother however, forced him to work and did not allow him to waste money. For instance, I had inherited a mill, the income of which was two tumans daily. My brother had a horse that required daily the same sum for its upkeep. I took the horse from my brother and in exchange gave him my mill and so the difference of two tumans daily was a gain for him but a loss for me. All other actions were the same kind and similar nature. Now you can easily make out the reason why." The man said: "Yes, it must be so, because his mother was a learned lady but yours ignorant." "Entertain honor with humility and poverty with patience." "A man must stand erect, not be kept erect by others." "It is more honorable to acknowledge our fault than to boast of our merits."

The second story is from the realm of a college graduate's personal experience. At the close of the public school and university career, his father became bankrupt, owing partially to the expense of giving his five sisters, two brothers and himself a costly education at home and abroad. Hence, he was compelled to face the world with nothing but the clothes he wore and an education—without experience, money and influence to step into. He was too theoretical to sell. In mathematics, he had been through algebra and trigonometry; in fact, he had reached the place where it was necessary to learn Greek and astronomy before proceeding any further. But, alas, he could not keep a set of books—the thing which a business man needed. Also, he had studied inorganic chemistry, though he had not the slightest intention of being a chemist! It was in the curriculum. Though he could quote formulas, solve equations, experiments in a laboratory with facility, he could not dispense or fill a prescription—the two capacities in which a chemist might need his services.

Thus he became a walking encyclopedia of useless academic knowledge and had nothing saleable to offer the business world. And now his position in the work-a-day world resembled that of a counterfeit coin in the realm of money—nobody wanted him. Finally he landed in New York where he went to work with a pick and shovel on an extension of the New York Subway alongside Italian laborers. With the work he had no particular fault to find. His fellow workmen were as good as he was, only their experience in life had been different. His chief anxiety was the lack of a social side to his life. For a while he liked to discuss art, literature and drama, current events at home and abroad and leading editorials. The men he was working with could not talk about the weather, the latest sporting news, etc. Thus, he became a social misfit. Then along came self-righteous people who pointed a finger of scorn at him and said, "Look at that man digging with a pick and shovel. I heard him lecture the other night on Greek philosophy. There must be something wrong with him; he had such a good education." They were wrong! He had never received any education at all, only instruction and scholarship—quite a different thing. He was merely a victim of that kind of college and school which is turning out men of this type by the thousands each year who unless backed by money and influence will never rise to a high degree. "Life is my college. May I graduate well, and earn some honor!" (*Alcott*). "He that hath a trade hath an estate."—*Franklin.*

One can imagine no more pathetic figure than that of the man who after leading a protected life at home and at church and school, arrives in the business world and social world with a firm belief in the things he has been taught, full of hope, high character, spirit and enterprise. If he lacks experience as is often the case in these days, the awakening is stupendous. This man was taught nothing about the world and its methods. His training had been very academic and therefore very narrow and unsuccessful. Aristiphus being asked what were the most necessary things for well born boys to learn, said, "Those things which they will put into practice when they become men."

"Experience is the child of thought, and thought is the child of action." We can not teach men from books.

Hippocrates (460-357 BC) said, "A physician should possess the following qualities: learning, wisdom, humanity, and probity (sincerity)." I believe that every educated man should possess these qualities. Horace Mann said, "If any man would seek for greatness, let him forget greatness and ask for truth and he will find both." About greatness read the following lines by C. E. Flynn:

"A man is as great as the dreams he dreams,
As great as the love he bears,
As great as the values he redeems,
And the happiness he shares.

A man is as great as the thoughts he thinks,
As the worth he has attained,
As the fountains at which his spirit drinks
And the insight he has gained.

A man is as great as the truth he speaks,
As great as the help he gives,
As great as the destiny he seeks,
As great as the life he lives."

Gladstone said "The disease of an evil conscience is beyond the practice of all the physicians of all the countries in the world."

About truth, Homer says, "Hateful to me as are the gates of hell is he who, hiding one thing in his heart, utters another." The antique Persians and Assyrians taught their children three useful things: to draw the bow, to ride and speak the truth. John Wycliffe wrote to the Duke of Lancaster "I believe that in the end the Truth will conquer." Yes, it conquered. Horace Mann also said, "Be ashamed to die until you have won some victory for humanity." Albert Schweitzer said, "I don't know what your destiny will be, but one thing I know, the only ones among you who will be really happy are those who will have sought and found how to serve." The slave Epictetus, who was born about the fiftieth year of our era and who was lame and deformed said, "Nothing is meaner than the love of pleasure, the love of gain, and insolence: nothing nobler than highmindedness, and nothing nobler than gentleness, and philanthropy, and doing good." When asked how a man could grieve his enemy, he replied: "By preparing to act in the noblest way." He also said, "If you wish to be good, first think and believe that you are bad."

"If you are going to do a good thing, do it now; if you are going to do a mean thing, wait till tomorrow." "To get good is human: to do good is human: to be good is divine." The old Saxon word "God" is identical with "good." God, "the good one," personified goodness— None loves God but he who loves good— "There is far more satisfaction in doing than in receiving good." (*Browning*). James said, "Therefore, he who knows to do good and does not do it, to him it is sin." I think the most heroic man I ever heard of was a poor clergyman with four pounds a week, who nursed a sick wife, did the housework, taught his two boys, provided free milk for destitute families, raised a fund to convert a tin church into a brick one, and kept hidden for two years the cancer that killed him.

There are many other stories of great sacrifice and courage. For the lack of space, I will mention only two of them:

A young doctor eight years ago had one kidney removed by surgical operation. The other kidney was damaged. His immediate relatives who were fit enough to give a kidney were of the wrong blood group. But another young doctor, hearing of his friend's critical position, gladly placed himself at his disposal. It was found that he possessed the same blood group, with the result that an operation was performed and a healthy kidney was transferred from his own body to the body of his friend.

The Rev. Reginald Banks reminds us of a scene in the streets of Aberdeen. Streets were lined with people, obviously disturbed and sad. All that was mortal of a washerwoman was going to its resting place. Among the mourners were many professional men, most of them doctors. Two particularly stood out. They were the two sons of the widow whose funeral it was. Both had the skillful hands of a surgeon and were men of high repute. Once they were poor lads in one of the poorest streets of the city. Their father died, and they needed money to finish their education. So the widowed mother, before the days of washing machines, took in washing. Day after day, and far into the night, she toiled to get the money to pay their fees. She won through, but at what a price! Her hands were twisted and gnarled, and her back bent by much stooping at the sink. When she lay cold in death, it was natural that the sons should look at her hands and then at their own. It follows in sequence of love that they kissed them, and murmured disjointedly, "She allowed her hands to be marred that ours might bring healing to others. Wonderful mother!"

In one of his fragments Epictetus tells the following anecdote. A person who had seen a poor ship-wrecked and almost dying pirate took pity on him, carried him home, gave him clothes and furnished him with all the necessities of life. Somebody reproached him for doing good to the wicked—"I have honored," he replied, "not the man, but humanity in his person."

"You give but little when you give of your possessions. It is when you give of yourself that you truly give." (*Khalil Jebran*).

> The lesson of St. Christopher
> Who spent his strength for others,
> And saved his soul by working hard
> To help and save his brothers. (*Jackson*)

> "Said Old gentleman Gay On a Thanksgiving day
> If you want a good time, then give something away."

> "A kind and gentle heart he had
> To comfort friends and foes:
> The naked everyday he clad
> When he put on his clothes." (*Goldsmith*)

> "That man may last, but never lives
> Who much receives but nothing gives."

"I have to live for others and not for myself: that is Middle Class morality." (*Shaw*).

The seven labors of mercy or more exactly the physical duties are: "To give food to the hungry, drink to the thirsty, clothe the naked, house strangers, release prisoners, visit the sick and bury the dead." (This lesson goes back to Matthew 25: 31-44.) Once Imperial Titus while having his supper reflected that he had done nothing for any that day. He broke out into that memorable and justly admired saying, "My friends, I have lost a day." "The vocation of every man and woman is to serve other people." (*Tolstoy*). "Do right to the widow, judge for the fatherless, give to the poor, defend the orphan, clothe the naked." (*Apoc*). "Be not weary in well doing." "Avoid as you would the plague a clergyman who is also a man of business." (*Jerome*). A noble deed is a step toward God.

> "There was a man, and some did count him mad,
> The more he gave away the more he had." (*Bunyan*)

Gladstone once said, "A gentleman is not a man who tries to get all he can out of life, but one who has a deep desire to contribute to life."

Walt Whitman said, "He or she is greatest who contributes the greatest original practical example." "Life is my college. May I graduate well, and earn some honor!" (*Alcott*). King George VI in his broadcast greeting after the coronation on May 12, 1935, said, "The highest of distinction is service to others." Oliver Cromwell (1599-1658), two days before his death, said, "I would be willing to live to be further service to God and His people but my work is done!" Yet God will be with his people. "For we do nothing but in the presence of two great witnesses—God and conscience."

"Pour forth all the odour, colour, charm and happiness you have to all your friends, to your home, to your daily society, to the poor and sorrowful, the joyous and the prosperous. Brighten darkened lives, soften the rude. Make a sunshine of peace in storm places, cover the faults and follies of men with the flower of love. Love others, and you will spread the delight of youth over all whom you meet and in doing so you will live intensely: for you will have within not only your own life, but also the lives of all whom you bless by love." (*Brooke*).

About service, it pleases me to mention the motto of the Rotary Club, "Service above self." Some other mottos are:

"We build"—*the Kiwanis Club*
"Love thy neighbor"—*the Modern Woodman*
"LABORARE EST ORARE" (To labor is to pray)—*motto of St. Benedict, founder of the Benedictine order*
"Be prepared"—*Boy Scouts*
"Look up and aim high"—*The Golden Star Brigade*
"Sacred thy body even as thy soul"—*Health and Strength League*
"Absolute honesty, absolute purity, absolute unselfishness, and absolute love"—*Frank Buchman of Oxford Group*
"Heart to God. Hand to man"—*Salvation Army*

"The beauty of the house is order:
The blessing of the house is contentment:
The glory of the house is hospitality:
The crown of the house is godliness."
Fireplace Motto

"Work as though you would live forever, live as though you would die today."—*our motto*

"Prefer diligence before idleness, unless you esteem rust before brightness." "Neither days nor lives can be made holy by doing nothing in them: the best prayer at the beginning of the day is that we may not lose its moments: the best grace before a meal, the consciousness that we have justly earned our dinner." (*Ruskin*). " 'Working is praying' said one of the holiest of men. And he spoke the truth; if a man but do his work from a sense of duty, which is for the sake of God." (*Kingsley*).

> "Like the star
> That shines afar,
> Without haste
> And without rest
> Let each man wheel with steady sway
> Round the task that rules the day,
> And do his best." (*Goethe*)

A Chinese proverb says "the nights are for dreams and the days are for fulfilling the dreams."

But there is no better motto which culture can have than these words of Bishop Wilson, "To make reason and the will of God prevail." It has been said that Alexander the Great came upon Diogenes as he searched among a pile of human bones. "What are you doing?" inquired Alexander. "I am looking for your father's bones, but I cannot tell them from the bones of his slaves." Once Goethe said, "If you inquire what the people are like here, I must answer that all men are the same everywhere." George Moore said, "After all there is but one race—humanity." Therefore, we want to understand that all men are alike basically and that everyone has need of the instruction given in these pages. Thomas Jefferson (1743-1826) put it, "all men are created equal; that they are endowed by this creator with certain inalienable rights; that among them are life, liberty and the pursuit of happiness." We ought not to lose opportunity in applying these fundamental questions. An opportunity is like a pin in the sweeping; you catch sight of it just as it flies away from you and gets buried again. "Nothing like the time present. Rest assured that a duty today done will be worth two duties saved for tomorrow." (*Spurgeon*). The famous Quaker, De Gullet, said, "I shall pass through the world but once; any good, therefore, that I can do and show to any human being, let me do it now. Let me not defer or neglect it, for I shall not pass this way again." Yes, everybody shall pass through this world but once and everything will pass away. "I came to the place of my birth and cried, 'The friends of my youth, where are they?' And echo answered, 'Where are they?'" (*Arabic Ms.*) At the time of his trial in England, Warren Hastings related to his friends an Indian tale which had given him much comfort. A monarch who suffered many hours of discouragement, urged his courtiers to devise a motto, short enough to be engraved on a ring, which should be suitable alike in prosperity and in adversity. After many suggestions had been rejected, his daughter offered an emerald bearing the inscription in Arabic: "Hatha Eidun Sayazool" (This, too, will pass.) Yes, everything will pass away.

> "Dead Petra in her hill-tomb sleeps,
> Her stones of emptiness remain;
> Around her sculptured mystery sweeps
> The lonely waste of Edom's plain." (Whittier)

"All that we see or seem: Is but a dream, within a dream." (Poe). "A fine quotation is a diamond on the finger of a man of wit, and a pebble in the hand of a fool." "The genius, wit and wisdom of a nation are discovered in its proverbs." (Bacon). "The tongue can no man tame, it is an unruly evil." Once Diogenes struck the father when the son swore. Sir Christopher Wren (1632-1723) gave the following notice to workmen employed during the building of St. Paul's Cathedral, London: "Whereas, among laborers and others, that ungodly custom of swearing is too frequently heard, to the dishonor of God and contempt of authority; and to the end that such impiety may be utterly banished from these workers, which are intended for the service of God and the honor of religion, it is ordered that profane swearing shall be a sufficient crime to dismiss any laborer."

Once Samuel Wesley with some literary friends was drinking coffee in one of London's coffee houses. A Colonel of Guards who sat at a nearby table was using blasphemous oaths. The young clergyman told the waiter, "Carry this glass of water to that gentleman in the red coat and ask him to wash his mouth after his oaths." Years later, the Colonel met Samuel in London and said to him, "Since that time, sir, I thank God I have feared an oath and everything that is offensive to the Divine Majesty." Samuel Wesley was born 300 years ago in England. He is overshadowed by his two famous sons, John and Charles. The work of John Wesley is well known, and Charles is well remembered for his hymns. At Christmas time literally thousands of voices sing, "Hark! the Herald Angels Sing."

James devoted a chapter of the Epistle to the subject of conduct of the tongue. J. Edwin Orr classifies the sins of the tongue as: "1) anger, 2) profanity, 3) lying, 4) criticism, 5) levity, 6) grumbling, 7) foul talk." Give your tongue more rest than your eyes and your ears. A Swiss inscription says, "Spechen ist silbern schweigen ist golden." "Speech is silver, silence is golden." Publius (42 BC) said, "I have often regretted my speech, never my silence." "Silence is deep as Eternity: speech is shallow as time." (Carlyle). "Rule tongue, temper, lust, and bridle the belly."

"I have learned silence from the talkative, toleration from the intolerant and kindness from the unkind: yet strange, I am ungrateful to those teachers." (Khalil Jebran).

"Speech finely framed delighteth the ears." (Apocrypha).

"A wise old owl sat on an oak
The more he saw the less he spoke:
The less he spoke the more he heard
Why aren't we like that wise old bird?" (Richards)

"Words are like leaves: and where they most abound
Much fruit of sense beneath is rarely found." (Pope)

"There are three kinds of silence, silence from words is good, because inordinate speaking tends to evil. Silence or rest from desires or passions is still better, because it promotes quietness of spirit. But the best of all is silence from unnecessary and wandering thought because that is essential to internal recollection, and because it lays a foundation for a proper regulation and silence in other respects." (Molinor). A single word has sometimes lost or won an empire—even less than a single word, if we believe the history of Darius's horse who proclaimed his master emperor without speaking—the seven candidates for the throne of Persia agreed that he should be king whose horse neighed first. The horse of Darius was the first.

This is the rule of the Harry Wadsworth Club:

"To look up and not down,
To look forward and not back,
To look out and not in, and
To lend a hand."

Therefore, let us keep our face always toward the sunshine and the shadows will fall behind us and let us all look up, aim high in our deeds delivering our words not in numbers, but in weight and not in quantity; but in quality, and let our speech which is a mirror of our soul be always with grace, seasoned with salt.

Part II

"Patch grief with Proverbs." (Shakespeare)

THE FEAR OF THE LORD IS THE BEGINNING OF WISDOM

A

ABILITY:
    No one knows what he can do till he tries.
    They can because they think they can (*Virgil*).
    Everyone excels in something in which another fails (*Latin*).

ABSENCE:
    Let no one be willing to speak ill of the absent.
    Absence sharpens love; presence strengthens it.
    Absence makes the heart grow fonder.
    Far from eye; far from heart.
    Distance sometimes endears friendship, and absence sweeteneth it.
    The absent party is still faulty.
    Never was the absent in the right.
    He that is absent is soon forgotten.
    Out of sight out of mind (*Homer*).
    Absence diminishes little passions and increases great ones.
    Friends though absent are still present (*Cicero*).
    Heart soon forgets what the eye sees not.
    Absence is the enemy of love.
    Our hours in love have wings; in absence, crutches (*Cibber*).

ABUNDANCE:
    Abundance makes poor.
    Abundance, like want, ruins man (*Franklin*).

ABUSE:
    The best things may be abused.

ACCIDENTS:
    Accidents will happen even in the best regulated families (*Dickens*).
    Nothing under the sun is accidental.

ACCUSING:
  Accusing is proving, when malice and force sit together.
ACQUAINTANCE:
  The more acquaintance, the more danger.
  More acquaintances less true friends.
  Short acquaintance brings repentance.
ACTION:
  Actions speak louder than words.
  Action is the proper fruit of knowledge.
  A crooked stick throws a crooked shadow.
  Great actions speak great minds.
  As you make your bed, so you must be on it.
  That action is best which procures the greatest happiness, for the greatest number (*Hutchinson*).
  He that sows thistles, shall reap prickers.
  He who sows the wind, shall reap the whirlwind.
  Such as a tree is, such is the fruit.
  Brave actions never want a trumpet.
  For the sake of one good action, a hundred evil ones should be forgotten (*Chinese*).
ADVANTAGE:
  Every advantage has its disadvantage.
ADVERSITY:
  Adversity makes a man wise, not rich.
  In the end things shall mend.
  You must be content sometimes with rough roads.
  You must take the fat with the lean.
  Adversity is the first path to truth (*Byron*).
  Gold is tried by fire; brave men by adversity (*Seneca*).
ADVICE:
  Advice none to marry or go to war.
  Advice comes too late when a thing is done.
  Advice whispered in the ear is worth a jeer.
  Too much consulting confounds.
  Better to ask than to go astray.
  Advice is something the wise don't need, and the fools won't take.
  Council is no command.
  Fools need advice most, but wise men only are the better for it (*Franklin*).
  Council must be followed, not praised.

Give neither council nor salt till you are asked for it.
Advice after mischief, is like medicine after death.
Nobody can give you wiser advice than yourself (*Cicero*).
Good advice is beyond price.
Teach your grandmother to sup yoghurt (sour milk) and to suck eggs.
If the council be good, no matter who gave it.
Give advice to all, but be security to none.
If you wish good advice, consult an old man.
Whatever advice you give, be brief (*Horace*).
It is safer to hear and take council than to give it.
Teach your father to get children.
Keep council to thyself first.
In giving advice, seek to help, not to please your friends.
Take your wife's first advice not her second.
Tell me something I don't know.
Though old and wise, you still need advice.
We may give advice, but we cannot give conduct.
Write down the advice of him who loves you though you like it not at present.
Advice whispered is not worth a cent.
He asks advice in vain who will not follow it.

AFFECTION:
Talk not about wasted affection; affection was not wasted (*Longfellow*).
As the rolling stone gathers no moss, so the roving heart gathers no affection (*Jameson*).

AFFLICTION:
Affliction, like the iron-smith, shapes and it smites.
The afflicted man is sacred (*Ovid*).

AFTER CAUTION:
It is too late to shut the stable after the horse is stolen.
It is too late to cast the anchor when the ship is on the rocks.
Everybody is wise after the event.
After-wit is fool's wit.
Age should think, and youth should do.

AFTER WISDOM:
Everybody is wise after the event.

AGE:
A man as he manages himself may be old at thirty, or young at eighty.

A head that is white, to maids brings no delight.
Every man at forty is a fool or a physician.
Old men for counsel, young men for war.
Men are as old as they feel; women are as old as they look.
A man is as old as his arteries.
The fewer his years, the fewer his tears.
The more your years, the nearer your grave.
It is hard to put old heads on young shoulders.
An old dog cannot alter his way of barking.
An old dog barks not in vain.
An old dog will learn no new tricks.
One is as old as one's heart.
An old sack asks much patching.
An old man is a bed full of bones.
Never too old to learn.
We do not count a man's years, until he has nothing else to count (*Emerson*).
Age is like love; it cannot be hid.
It is always in season for the old to learn.
No wise man ever wished to be young.
The hell of women is old age.
Old age plants more wrinkles in the mind than in the face. (*Montague*).
Old people see best in the distance.
Women and music should never be dated.
An old fox understands a trap.
Nobody loves life like an old man.
Age steals away all things, even the mind (*Virgil*).
The old age of an eagle is better than the young of a sparrow.
Life is most delightful when it is on the downward slope. (*Seneca*).
In youth and strength, think of age and weakness.
An angelic boyhood becomes a satanic old age (*Erasmus*).
Age like distance lends a double charm (*Oliver Wendell Holmes*).
No one is so old as to think he cannot live one more year. (*Cicero*).
Old age makes us wiser and more foolish.
Who steals an old man's supper does him no harm.
When the age is in, the wit is out (*Shakespeare*).
Youth is a blunder; manhood a struggle; old age a regret.
An old ox makes a straight furrow.
Old age is a tyrant who forbids, upon pain of death, all pleasure of youth (*La Rouchefoucauld*).

AGREEMENT:
: Fools bite one another, but wise men agree together.
ALMOST:
: Almost never killed a fly.
ALMS:
: Alms are the golden keys that open the gates of heaven.
: Alms never make poor.
: Alms giving never made any man poor, nor robbers rich, nor prosperity wise.
ALONE:
: A man alone is either a saint or a devil (*Burton*).
: Loneliness is worshipping.
: It is not good to be alone even in Paradise.
: Better be alone than in bad company.
AMBITION:
: The trap to the highborn is ambition.
: Ambition is the only proof that combats love (*Cibber*).
: Ambition obeys no law but its own appetite.
: I would rather be the first man here, than the second at Rome (*Caesar*).
: He that never climbed, never fell.
: Fling away ambition. By that sin fell the angels (*Shakespeare*).
: Would you rise in the world, veil ambition with the forms of humanity (*Chinese*).
AMERICA:
: America means opportunity, freedom, power (*Emerson*).
: Equal rights for all, special privileges for none. (*Jefferson*).
AMUSEMENT:
: Amusement is the happiness of those who do not think.
ANCESTRY:
: I don't know who my grandfather was: I am much more concerned to know who his grandson will be (*Lincoln*).
: High buildings have a low foundation.
: He who serves well his country has no need of ancestors (*Voltaire*).
: He is well-born who is by nature well-fitted for virtue (*Seneca*).
ANGER:
: An angry man stirreth up strife (*Proverbs*).
: He that is angry without a cause must be pleased without amends.
: Anger resteth in the bosom of fools (*Proverbs*).
: He that is slow to wrath is of great understanding (*Proverbs*).
: "Anger is the parent of Murder." (*Billy Graham*)

Let not the sun go down upon your wrath (Proverbs).
A man in a passion rides a mad horse.
Anger and haste hinders a good council.
Anger is never without reason, but seldom a good one.
Anger may glance into the heart of a wise man, but only rests in the bosom of a fool (Seneca).
Anger punishes itself.
Beware of the fury of a patient man.
The dog bites the stone, not him that throws it.
When angry count ten and hundred.
Anger is a short madness (Horace).
Anger manages everything badly (Stateus).
Fury and anger carry the mind away (Virgil).
However weak the hand anger gives it strength.
The greatest remedy for anger is delay.
Anger begins with folly and ends with repent.

ANSWER:
Who answers suddenly knows little.
A soft answer turneth away wrath (Proverbs).
No answer is also an answer.
Not all words require an answer.
Silence is often the best answer.
The shortest answer is doing.

ANT:
No worker better than the ant, and she says nothing.

ANTIQUITY:
Antiquity is not always a mark of verity.

APOLOGIES:
Apologies only account for that which they do not alter.

APPEARANCE:
A black plum is as sweet as the white.
Appearances are deceptive.
Don't judge a tree by its bark.
Do not look upon the vessel, but upon that which it contains.
Better cut the shoe than pinch the foot.
The fairest looking shoe may pinch the foot.
Judge not according to the appearance.
Good swords have often been in poor scabbards.
Look to the mind, not to the outward appearance.
You can't judge the horse by the harness.
All that glitters is not gold.

APPETITE:
> Put a knife to thy throat if thou be a man given to appetite (Proverbs).
> Seek an appetite by hard toil.
> Poor men want meat for their stomachs; rich men stomach for their meat.
> He who checks his appetite avoids death (Chinese).
> There is no stomach a hands' breadth bigger than another.

APPLE:
> All the evil in the world was brought in by an apple.
> An apple a day keeps the doctor away.
> The best apple is eaten by the bear.
> What is good of a red apple if it has a worm.
> The apples on the other side of the wall are the sweetest.

ARCHER:
> A good archer is not known by his arrow, but by his aim.

ARCHITECTURE:
> Houses are built to live in, not to look on (Bacon).
> When we build, let us think that we build forever (Ruskin).
> Every man is the architect of his own fortune.

ARGUMENT:
> Do not investigate facts by the light of the arguments, but arguments by the light of the facts (Greek).
> In a heated argument we are apt to lose sight of the truth.
> A noisy man is always in the right.
> You have not converted a man because you have silenced him.

ARMAMENTS:
> One sword keeps the other in the sheath.

ARMS:
> Arms carry peace.
> Arms and money require good hands.

ARMY:
> Two armies are two bodies which meet and try to frighten each other (Napoleon).
> An army, like a serpent, goes on its belly. (Napoleon).

ART:
> Art is a shadow of divine perfection (Michelangelo).
> Nature is the art of God (Dante).
> Art is long, life is short (Hippocrates).
> All the arts are the brothers; each one is a light to the other (Voltaire).

Art has an enemy called ignorance.
As the sun colours the flowers, so thus art colours life.

ARTIST:
A good painter can draw a devil as well as an angel.
Every artist writes his own autobiography.
An artist lives everywhere.

ASKING:
A good asker needs a good listener.
Do not ask for what you will wish you had not got. (Seneca).
He that is too proud to ask is too proud to receive.
Better ask ten times, than go astray once.
The highest price a man can pay for a thing is to ask for it.
Asking costs little.
When a friend asks, there is no tomorrow.

ASPIRATION:
He that stays in the valley shall never get over the hill.
Hitch your wagon to a star (*Emerson*).
The scene changes, but the aspiration of men of good will persists (*Beech*).

ASS:
An ass is but an ass, though laden with gold.
An ass loaded with gold climbs to the top of a castle.
An ass often carries gold on his back, yet feeds on the thistles.
What good can it do an ass to be called a lion?
An ass must be tied where the master will have him.
An ass that carries a load is better than a lion that devours men.
I had rather aid an ass that carries me than a horse that throws me.

ATHEISM:
Atheism is rather in the lips than in the heart of people (*Bacon*).
By night, an atheist half believes in God.
Some are atheists in fair weather.

AUCTION:
At an auction keep your mouth shut.

AVARICE:
Money lies nearest them that are nearest their graves (*Wm. Penn*).
He that grasps at too much holds nothing fast.
It is not want but abundance that makes avarice.
He that will have all loveth all.
Avarice is the root of all evil.
Avarice is the vice of declining years.

B

BABY:
A baby is an angel whose wings decrease as his legs increase.

BACHELOR:
An old bachelor is only the half of a pair of scissors.

BAD:
A bad thing never dies.
Bad men leave their mark wherever they go (*Chinese*).
A bad tree does not yield good apples.
What is bad for one is good for another.
Into the mouth of a bad dog often falls a good bone.
Bad mind, but good heart.
Nothing is so bad as not to be good for something.

BALANCE:
Every hill has its valley.
Every light has its shadow.
Every tide has its ebb.
There is no summer, but it has a winter.
You can't eat your cake, and have it too.
If you sell the cow, you will sell her milk with her.

BARBER:
Barber learns to shave of shaving fools.

BARGAIN:
On a good bargain, think twice.
It takes two to make a bargain.

BARK:
Barking dogs never bite.
His bark is worse than his bite.

BASHFULNESS:
Bashfulness is an enemy of poverty.

BEARD:
It is not the beard that makes the philosopher.
He is false by nature that has a black head and a red beard.

BEAUTY:
Beauty is the gift of God (*Aristotle*).
What is beautiful is good, and who is good will soon also be beautiful.
Beauty is a natural superiority. (*Plato*)
As a jewel of gold in a swine's mouth, so is a fair woman who is without discretion.
A fair woman without virtue is like palled wine.

A fair face may be a foul bargain.
A fair face may hide a foul heart.
Beauty and wisdom are rarely conjoined.
A fine woman can do without fine clothes.
Rare is the union of beauty and modesty.
Over the greatest beauty hangs the greatest ruin.
Beautiful flowers are soon picked.
Beauty is a fading flower (*Prov.*).
An enemy to beauty is a foe to nature.
Beauty is a short lived reign.
Beauty blemished once forever lost (*Shakespeare*).
Beauty is but skin deep.
Beauty is but a blossom.
Beauty is the flower of virtue.
Beauty and honesty seldom agree.
Beauty without virtue is a flower without perfumes.
Beauty and folly are old companions.
Beauty has no inheritance.
We seize the beautiful and reject the useful.
Beauty opens locked doors.
The fairest rose is soonest withered.
All heiresses are beautiful.
The handsomest flower is not the sweetest.
Dear to the heart of girls is their own beauty (*Ovid*).
Beauty has wings and too hastily flies.
Beauty may have fair leaves, but little fruit.
Beauty is another's good.
The perception of beauty is a moral test (*Thoreau*).

BED:
Early to bed and early to rise, makes a man healthy, wealthy, and wise (*Franklin*).
As you make your bed, so you must lie on it.
Bed is a medicine.

BEG:
Who is not ashamed to beg soon is not ashamed to steal.
Better is to die than to beg (*Apocrypha*).
Better to beg than to steal, but better to work than beg.

BEGGARS:
Beggars breed and rich men feed.
If wishes were horses, beggars might ride.
Beggars fear no rebellion.

Beggars can never be bankrupt.
It is better to be a beggar than to be foul.
Beggars mounted run their horses to death.
Beggar is jealous of beggar.
Gifts make beggars bold.
The beggar's wallet has no bottom.

BEGINNINGS:
Beware beginnings (Greek).
The beginnings of all things are small (Cicero).
A good beginning is half the battle.
Everything is difficult at first.
He that begins many things finishes but few.
All glory comes from daring to begin.
Good beginning makes good ending.
Better never begin than never make an end.
A bad beginning makes a bad ending.
Each goodly thing is hardest to begin (Spencer).
For a web begun, God sends thread.
Everything must have a beginning.
Well begun is half done.

BEHAVIOR:
Let every man be swift to hear, slow to speak.
Walk grandly, talk profoundly, drink roundly, sleep soundly.
Behavior is the mirror in which everyone shows his image (Goethe).
If not seemly, do it not: if not true, say it not (Greek).
Bad conduct soils the finest ornament more than filth.

BELIEVE:
Believe not all you hear, and tell not all you believe.
We soon believe what we desire.
Blessed are they that have not seen and yet have believed.
They can conquer who believe they can.
Who knows much believes the less.
Who quick believes late repents.

BELL:
When the great bells are ringing no one heard the little ones.
Bells call others, but themselves enter not the church.

BELLY:
The belly carries the legs, and not the legs the belly (Spanish).
An empty belly hears nobody.
Better fill a man's belly than his eye.

No belly is filled with fair words.
No clock is more regular than the belly.
When the belly is full, the mind is amongst the maids.
It is hard to argue with the belly since it has no ears (*Cato*).
A full belly is the mother of all evil.
The belly is a bad advisor.

BEND:
Better bend than break.

BENEFITS:
Write benefits in marble, injuries in dust (*Franklin*).
Benefits turn poison in bad minds.
Benefits, like flowers, please most when they are first.
The last benefit is the most remembered.
He who confers a benefit on anyone loves him better than he is beloved (*Aristotle*).
There is no grace in a benefit that sticks to the fingers.
Good that comes too late is good as nothing.
When befriended, remember it; when you be friend forget it (*Franklin*).
Benefits are only agreeable as long as one can repay them.

BEST SIDE, LOOKING ON THE:
Look rather on the good of evil men than on the evil of good men.
Best is best.
The best is cheapest.
The best things in life are free.

BETTER:
Better half an egg than an empty shell.
Better to wear out than to rust out.
Better be the head of a cat, than the tail of a lion.
Better an ugly face than a black heart.
Better a bare foot than none at all.

BEWARE:
Beware of no man more than of thyself.

BIRDS:
Birds of a feather flock together.
The early bird catches the worm.
Birds of prey do not sing.

BIRTH:
Our birth made us mortal, our death will make us immortal.
Naked was I born, naked I am; I neither lose nor gain (*Cervantes*).

BITTER:
    Bitter pills may have sweet effects.
    Who has never tasted what is bitter does not know what is sweet.
BLACK:
    He that wears black must hang a brush at his back.
    Above black there is no color.
    Above salt there is no savor.
BLESSINGS:
    Blessings are not valued till they are gone.
    Out of the same mouth proceedeth blessing and cursing.
    Blessed is he that comes in the name of the lord.
BLINDNESS:
    When the blind man carries the banner, woe to those who follow.
    A blind man will not thank you for a looking glass.
    A pebble and a diamond are alike to a blind man.
    What matters to a blind man that his father could see.
    The eyes are blind when the mind is elsewhere.
    In the kingdom of blind men, the one eyed is king.
    Among the blind close your eyes.
BLOOD:
    Human blood is all of one colour.
    Send your noble blood to market and see what it will buy.
BOAST:
    He that boasts of his own knowledge proclaims his ignorance.
    The greatest boasters are not the greatest doers.
    Great boasters, little doers.
    Believe a boaster as you would a liar.
    A boaster and a liar are cousins.
BODY:
    A little body often harbors a great soul.
    If any thing is sacred, the human body is sacred (*Whitman*).
BONE:
    Bones for those who come late.
BOOK:
    A book that remains shut is but a block.
    Books must follow sciences, and not sciences books (*Bacon*).
    Something is learned every time a book is opened.
    A wicked book is the wickedest because it cannot repent.
    Books are the blessed choloroform of the mind.
    Books are the children of the brain.

Books are for wisdom, piety, delight, or use (*Denham*).
Books are a guide in youth, and an entertainment for old age.
Have thy study full of books, than thy purse full of money.
No furniture so charming as books.
Judge not a book by its cover.
Books are ships which pass through the vast seas of time (*Bacon*).
A room without books is a body without a soul.
A good book is the precious life-blood of a master spirit (*Milton*).
Books and friends should be few and good.
The best companions are the best books.
The most lasting monuments.
The books which help you the most are those which make you think the most (*Parker*).
Wear the old coat and buy the new book.

BORROWING:
Better buy than borrow.
He that borrows must pay again with shame or loss.
A borrowed cloak does not keep warm.
He that goes a-borrowing goes a-sorrowing.
The borrower is the servant of the lender (*Prov.*).
Neither a borrower nor a lender be (*Shakespeare*).
Creditors have better memories than debtors.
Borrowing is not much better than begging.
Borrowed garments never fit well.

BOUGH:
The boughs that bear most hang lowest.

BOY:
A growing youth has a wolf in his belly.
Boys will be men one day.

BRAIN:
An empty brain is the devil's shop.
If the brain sows not corn, it plants thistles.
Half the brain is enough for him who says little.

BRAVE:
All are brave when the enemy flies.
None but the brave deserve the fair (*Dryden*).
To a brave man, every soil is his country (*Ovid*).

BREAD:
Cast thy bread upon the waters, for thou shalt find it after many days (*Eccl.*).
Give us this day our daily bread (*Matt.*).

Man shall not live by bread alone.
Eaten bread is forgotten.

BREEDING:
Better unborn than unbred.
Vipers breed vipers.
Bad bird, bad egg.
Prey bird is known by its beak.

BREVITY:
Use not vain repetitions (Matt.).
Let thy speech be short, comprehending much in few words (Apoc.).
It is better to be brief than tedious (Shakespeare).
Brevity is the soul of wit (Shakespeare).

BRIBES:
Bribes throw dust in cunning men's eyes.
A greased mouth cannot say no.
Bribes will enter without knocking.
Honesty stands at the gate and knocks, and bribery enters in.
Bribery and theft are first cousins.
Few men have virtue to withstand the highest bidder (Washington).

BRIDE:
The weeping bride makes a laughing wife.
If every one seeks a handsome bride what will become of the ugly ones.
At the wedding feast, the least eater is the bride.

BROOM:
As a man needs clothes, so a house needs a broom.
A new broom sweeps clean.

BROTHER:
Let brotherly love continue.
A brother is a friend given by nature.

BUILD:
The stone which the builders refused is become the head stone of the corner (Ps.).
No good building without a good foundation.
It is easier to pull down than to build.

BURDEN:
Bear ye one another's burdens.
In a long journey straw weighs.

Every horse thinks his own pack heaviest.
No one knows the weight of another's burden.

BUSINESS:
Business is business.
Seest thou a man diligent in his business? He shall stand before kings (*Prov.*).
Keep thy shop and thy shop will keep thee.
A man without a smiling face should not open a shop.
Every one knows his own business.
Business before pleasure.
The market is a place set apart where men may deceive each other.

BUSY:
Some are always busy and never do anything.
To the boiling pot the flies come not.
As busy as a bee.
None so busy as those who do nothing.

BUYING AND SELLING:
It is not a sin to sell dear, but it is to make ill measure.
Buyers want a hundred eyes; sellers none.
Ask much to have little.
There are more foolish buyers than foolish sellers.

C

CAGE:
A golden cage won't feed the bird.

CAKE:
You can't have your cake and eat it.
Every cake has its maker.

CALAMITY:
Calamity is the touchstone of a brave mind.

CANDLE:
Neither do men light a candle and put it under a basket (*Matt.*).
Choose neither a woman nor linen by candle-light.
At the foot of the candle it is dark.
The candle does not give light to itself.

CANDOR:
Speak boldly and speak truly to shame the devil.
There is no wisdom like frankness.

CARDS:
Cards are the devil's prayer book.

CARE:
Care and fine stable make a good horse.
Want of care admits despair.

CARELESSNESS:
Careless shepherds make many a feast for the wolf.

CATS:
Never was a mewing cat a good mouser.
When a cat and mouse agree the former has no chance.
When the cat is away the mice will play.

CAUSES:
A man is a lion in his own cause.
Zeal in a good cause is commendable.
He that has the worst cause makes the worst noise.
A bad cause will be supported by bad men.
They never fail who die in a great cause (Byron).
Most are blind in their own cause.

CAUTION:
Think before you act.
He that looks not before, finds himself behind.
Lock the stable before the horse is stolen.
Look before you leap.

CERTAINTY:
A feather in hand is better than a bird in bush.
Be not ashamed to say what you are not ashamed to think (Montaigne).
Better an egg today than two to-morrow.
Speak out; hide not thy thoughts (Homer).
Nothing is certain but death and taxes.

CHARACTER:
Character is the diamond that scratches every other stone.
The best way to teach character is to have it around the house.

CHARITY:
Charity begins at home.
He that feeds upon charity has a cold dinner and no supper.
The charitable give out at the door and God puts in at the window.
Great almsgiving lessens no man's living.

CHASTITY:
Who can find a virtuous woman; for her price is far above rubies (Prov.).

CHEAP:
> The best is cheapest.
> The cheap is dear.

CHEERFUL:
> A cheerful look makes a dish a feast.
> Cheerfulness is medicine for the mind.
> Cheerful company shortens the miles.
> Be merry and wise.

CHILDREN:
> Suffer the little children to come to me, for to such is the Kingdom of Heaven.
> Our neighbor's children are always the worse.
> Give a child his will and he will turn out ill.
> Children and drunkards speak truth.
> Train up a child the way he should go.
> Children are poor men's riches.
> Late children, early orphans.
> Let the child's first lesson be obedience.
> Children and fools have merry lives.
> Children are the keys of paradise.
> Better the child should cry than the father.
> He that does not beat his child will later beat his own breast.
> When children stand still, they have done some ill.
> Children suck the mother when they are young, and the father when grown up.
> How sharper than a serpent's tooth it is to have a thankless child (Shakespeare).

CHURCH:
> All are not saints that go to church.
> The churches must learn humility as well as teach it.
> Many come to bring their clothes to church rather than themselves.

CITY:
> Unless the Lord keepeth the city, the watchman waketh in vain.
> Cities should be walled with the courage of their dwellers (Greek).
> A great city a great solitude.
> A city that is set on a hill cannot be hid.
> Do not dwell in a city whose governor is a physician.

CIVILIZATION:
> Civilization degrades the many to exalt the few (Alcott).
> Civilization is the making of civil persons (Ruskin).

CLEANLINESS:
    Cleanliness is next to godliness.
    Cleanliness is the key to prayer.
    Have not only clean hands but clean minds.
    Cleanliness is from faith.
CLIMB:
    He who would climb the ladder must begin at the bottom.
CLOAK:
    Under a good cloak may be a bad man.
CLOTHES:
    Good clothes open all doors.
    Till April death, change not a thread.
CLOUD:
    After black clouds, clean weather.
    If you do not enter a tiger's den, you cannot get his cubs.
    One cloud is enough to eclipse all the sun.
COCK:
    A cock is bold on his own dunghill.
COMFORTABLE:
    He that is warm thinks all so.
COMMAND:
    There is great force hidden in a sweet command.
    Command your temper, lest it command you.
    He that cannot obey cannot command.
COMMON SENSE:
    Better short of pence than short of sense.
COMPANY:
    Tell me with whom you go, and I will tell you what you are.
    A wicked companion invites us all to hell.
    A merry companion is music in a journey.
    He is known by his companions.
    Better be alone than in bad company.
    Evil communications corrupt good manners.
    We know a man by the company he keeps.
    If you live with a lame person you will learn to limp.
    Better fare hard with good men, than feast with bad.
    Keep not ill men company, lest you increase the number.
    He who goes with wolves will learn to howl.
    No road is long with good company.
COMPENSATION:
    On the fall of an oak every man gathers wood.

COMPLIMENTS:
   Compliments cost nothing; yet many pay dear for them.
COMPROMISE:
   Stretch your legs according to the length of your quilt.
CONCEIT:
   Conceit is the finest armour a man can wear.
   She holds up her head like a hen drinking.
CONFESSION:
   Confess and be hanged.
   Open confession is good for the soul.
   A generous confession disarms slander.
   Confess your sins and the Lord is ever ready to forgive them.
CONQUER:
   Conquer thyself.
   He that will conquer must fight.
   He is twice the conqueror who can restrain himself in the hour of victory.
CONSCIENCE:
   Keep conscience clean, then never fear.
   Value a good conscience more than praise.
   A good conscience is a soft pillow.
   A clean conscience is a good card.
   Conscience is the voice of God in the soul.
   A good conscience is the best divinity.
   A clean conscience is a wall of brass.
   A guilty conscience needs no accuser.
   He that has no conscience has nothing.
   No hell like a bad conscience.
   An evil conscience breaks many a man's neck.
   A man's conscience tells him what is honour.
   A bad conscience is a snake in one's heart.
CONTEMPT:
   Contempt will sooner kill an injury than revenge.
CONTENT:
   Take things as they come.
   He who is content can never be ruined.
   When we have not what we like, we must like what we have.
   He that cannot get meat must be content with cabbage.
   Content is everlasting treasure.
CONVENTION:
   When you are in Rome do what the Romans do.

COOK:
> Too many cooks spoil the broth.

CORN:
> In good years corn is hay; in ill years straw the corn.

COST:
> One cannot make the pancakes without breaking eggs.
> The more cost the more honor.

COUNSEL:
> Good counsel has no price.
> If the counsel be good no matter who gave it.
> Good counsel never comes too late.
> Though you are a prudent man, do not despise counsel.

COUNT:
> Count not your chickens before they are hatched.

COUNTRY:
> I only regret that I have only one life to lose for my country (*Hale*).

COURAGE:
> A gallant man needs no drums to rouse him.
> If you do not enter a tiger's den, you cannot get his cubs.
> A valiant man's look is more than a coward's sword.
> Where there is a brave man, there is the thickest of the fight.
> A man of courage never wants weapons.
> All are brave when the enemy flies.
> Faint heart never won fair lady.
> Fortune favors the brave.
> The test of courage is to bear defeat, without losing heart.
> It is courage that wins, and not good weapons.
> An ill cook cannot lick his own fingers.
> The brave are born from the brave.
> Courage is that virtue which champions the cause of right.

COURTESY:
> Courtesy costs nothing.
> All doors open to courtesy.
> Lip honor costs little, yet many bring in much.

COW:
> The old cow thinks she never was a calf.

COWARD:
> A coward calls himself cautious and a miser thrifty.
> The coward threatens only when he is safe.
> To see what is right and not to do it, is the part of a coward.

Cowards do not count in battle; they are there but not in it.
Cowards are cruel.
Cowardice is the mother of cruelty.
CRIME:
Crime may be secret yet not secure.
No crime is founded upon reason.
CROOKED:
Crooked iron may be strengthened with the hammer.
CRY:
It is no use crying over spilled milk.
CURE:
Good language cures great sores.
What can't be cured must be endured.
CURSES:
Curses are devil's language.
CUSTOM:
Break the legs of an evil custom.
CUT:
Cut not the bough that thou standest upon.

D

DANCE:
The greater the fool, the better the dancer.
Dancing is the child of music and love.
It was surely the devil who taught women to dance.
DANGER:
Danger past, God forgotten.
After the greatest danger, the greatest pleasure.
Where there is no danger, there is no glory.
Dangers are overcome by dangers.
The more danger the more honour.
Sweet is danger.
DARKNESS:
Men loved darkness more than light, because their deeds were evil (*John*).
DAUGHTER:
He who has daughters is always a shepherd.
Marry your son when you will, your daughter when you can.
Judge the daughter by the mother.
He that would the daughter win, must with the mother first begin.

Who does not beat his daughters, will one day strike his knees in vain.

A daughter married is a daughter lost.

DAY:

A bad day had never a good night.

Every day in my life is a leaf in the history.

The day has eyes, the night has ears.

Every day brings its bread with it.

Think in the morning, act in the noon, eat in the evening, sleep in the night (*Blake*).

DEAD:

Speak not of a dead man at the table.

If you slander a dead man you stab him in the grave.

DEATH:

The righteous man hath hope in his death (*Ps.*).

Make little weeping for the dead, for he is at rest (*Apocrypha*).

As soon as a man is born he begins to die.

Death is but a path that must be trod.

Speak nothing but good of the dead.

Death will seize the doctor too.

Let the dead bury the dead.

For dust thou art, and into dust shall thou return.

Few have luck, all have death.

Let me die the death of the righteous.

The Lord gave, and the Lord hath taken away; blessed be the name of the Lord (*Job*).

O death, where is thy sting? O grave, where is thy victory?

Death makes equal the high and the low.

Whom God lovest best, these he taketh soonest.

A man can die but once; we owe God a death (*Shakespeare*).

We all do fade as a leaf.

Death takes no bribes.

Gold, lads, and girls, all must, as chimney-sweepers, come to dust. (*Shakespeare*).

Yea, though I walk through the valley of the shadow of death, I shall fear no evil.

He that died half a year ago is as dead as Adam.

It is as natural to die as to be born.

Happy he who dies before he calls for death to take him away.

He that fears death lives not.

We weep when we are born, not when we die.

41

The good die early and the bad die late.
Six feet of earth makes all men equal.
The life of the death is in the memory of living.
Him who is dead, honor with remembrance, not with tears.
There is no cure for birth and death save to enjoy the interval (Santayana).
Remember you must die.
Old men go to death, but death comes to young men.

DEBT:
Owe no man anything, but to love one another (Rom.).
A little debt makes a debtor, but a great one an enemy.
He that gets out of debt grows rich.
Rather go to bed supperless than rise in debt.
Debtors are liars.
Out of debt out of danger.
Debt is the worst poverty.

DECEIT:
Let no man deceive you with vain words (Eph).
If a man deceives me once shame on him, if twice, shame on me.
It is my own fault if I am deceived by the same man twice.

DECENCY:
A clean fast is better than a dirty breakfast.

DECISION:
Swift decisions are not sure.

DEED:
Handsome is that handsome does.
Deeds are fruits, words are leaves.
A noble deed is a step toward God.
Every man is the son of his own works.
If you have done a good deed, boast not of it.
Deeds not words.
Let us do or die (Bacon).
Our deeds are sometimes better than our thoughts.
The reward of a good deed is to have done it.
A good man makes no name of a good deed.

DELAY:
Delays are dangerous.
We have delay, yet it makes us wise.
Don't delay today's work for tomorrow.
A delay is better than a disaster.

DELIBERATION:
> Affairs like salt fish ought to be a good while soaking.
> Great designs require great consideration.

DENIALS:
> A fault once denied is twice committed.
> Denials make little faults great.

DEPENDENCE:
> He who depends on another, dines ill or sups worse.

DESIRE:
> Humble hearts have humble desires.

DESPAIR:
> Despair gives courage to a coward.
> Despair has often gained battles.
> Never despair (Horace).

DEVIL:
> The devil is the father of lies.
> Renounce the devil and all his works.
> Resist the devil and he will flee from you (James).
> The prince of darkness is a gentleman (Shakespeare).
> The devil can cite scriptures for his purpose (Shakespeare).
> The devil is never far off.
> If the devil catch a man idle, he will set him to work.
> Talk of the devil and he will appear.

DIAMOND:
> A diamond is valuable though it lie on a dunghill.
> Diamonds cut diamonds.

DIET:
> Diet plays a helpful part.

DIFFICULTY:
> Difficulty is the daughter of idleness.
> Nothing is difficult to a willing mind.
> The hard things are the most difficult.

DIGNITY:
> The easiest way to dignity is humility.

DILIGENCE:
> Seest thou a man diligent in his business? He shall stand before Kings (Prov.).

DINNER:
> After dinner sit a while, after supper walk a mile.
> Better is a dinner of herbs where love is, than a stuffed lamb and hated therewith.

DISCORD:
If a house be divided against itself, that house cannot stand.
DISCRETION:
Discreet women have neither eyes nor ears.
DISEASE:
A disease known is half cured.
Disease will have its course.
To hide disease is fatal.
DISPUTES:
In too much dispute truth is lost.
Use soft words and hard arguments.
DISSIMULATION:
The devil can quote scriptures when he sees need for it.
DIVORCE:
Divorce is the public brand of shameful life.
DO:
If you would have a thing well done, do it yourself.
They that do nothing learn to do ill.
When a thing is done, make the best of it.
DOCTOR:
Do to others as you would like others to do to you.
An ignorant doctor is no better than a murderer (*Chinese*).
Beware of the young doctor, and the young barber.
God heals, and the doctor takes the fee.
He is the best physician who knows the worthlessness of most medicines.
Honor a physician before thou hast need of him.
If the doctor cures the sun sees it; if he kills the earth hides it.
Every man at thirty is either a fool or a physician.
DOGS:
A dog will not cry if you beat him with a bone.
Dogs that bark at a distance never bite.
An old dog cannot change the way of barking.
Beware of silent dog and still water.
The dog barks and the caravan passes.
DOING:
Better do it than wish it done.
That which is worth doing is worth doing well.
We do nothing but in the presence of two great witnesses—God and Conscience.

DREAM:
: All men of action are dreamers.
DRESS:
: Clothes make the man.
: Dress does not give knowledge.
: Eat to please thyself, but dress to please others.
: Fine feathers make fine birds.
: Good clothes open doors.
: In your own country your name, in other countries your dress.
DRINK:
: The devil is behind the glass.
DROWNING:
: A drowning man will catch at a straw.
DRUNKENNESS:
: Woe unto them that rise up early in the morning, that they may follow strong drink (*Isaiah*).
: When the wine is in, the wit is out.
: Choose thy company before thy drink.
: Thousands drink themselves to death before one dies of thirst.
: The devil is behind the glass.
: Wisdom is clouded by wine.
: A drunkard's purse is a bottle.
: Drunkenness makes some men fools, some beasts, and some devils.
: A drunken night makes a cloudy morning.
: Drunkenness is voluntary madness.
: The drunkard is always talking of wine.
: Drunkenness turns a man out of himself, and leaves a beast in his room.
: What soberness conceals, drunkenness reveals.
DUPLICITY:
: May the man be damned and never grow fat who wears two faces under one hat.
DUST:
: He that blows in the dust fills his eyes with it.
DUTY:
: Duty before pleasure.
: Duty is what one expects from others (*O. Wilde*).
: Stern daughter of the voice of God (*Wordsworth*).
: It is an honour to have remembered one's duty.
: Duty determines destiny.

E

EAGLE:
    No need to teach an eagle to fly.
    Eagles fly alone.
    When the eagle is dead, the crows pick out his eyes.

EAR:
    The ear trieth words and the mouth tasteth meat (*Job*).
    Give every man thy ear, but few thy voice (*Shakespeare*).
    Walls have ears.
    Cities are taken by ears.
    We have two ears and one mouth, that we may listen the more and talk the less.
    Ears are eyes to the blind (*Greek*).
    In at one ear, and out at the other.
    If your ear "rings" some one is talking or thinking of you.
    One pair of ears draws a hundred tongues.

EARLY:
    Early to bed and early to rise, makes a man healthy, wealthy and wise.
    The early bird catches the worm.
    The morning hour has gold in its mouth.
    He that will thrive, must rise at five,
    He that had thriven may lie till seven.
    And he that will never thrive may lie till eleven.
    Early to bed and early to get married.

EARTH:
    The earth is the Lord's, and the fulness thereof (*Ps.*).
    Earth is the best shelter.
    The earth is a host who murders his guests.

EAST:
    Oh, East is East, and West is West, and never the twain shall meet (*Kipling*).

EASY:
    As easy as lying.
    It is easier to pull down than to build up.

EAT:
    Eat to live, and not live to eat.
    Take no thought for your life, or what you shall eat, or what you shall drink (*Matt.*).
    Where therefore, ye eat, or drink, or whatever ye do, do all to the glory of God (*I Cor.*).

Gather up the fragments that remain that nothing is lost.
By suppers more have been killed than Galen ever cured.
To lengthen thy life, lessen the meals.
It is good to be merry at meat.
He that eats well should do his duty well.
Tell me what you eat, and I will tell you what you are.
Many dishes make many diseases.
Not with whom you are bred, but with whom you are fed.
Eat enough and it will make you wise.
Young children and chickens would ever be eating.
A man may dig his grave with his teeth.
What is good to one may be poison to another.
He who eats too much knows not how to eat.
The table robs more than the thief.
The proof of the pudding is in the eating.
Eat at pleasure, drink by measure.
There's no love more sincere than the love of food.

ECONOMY:
Take care of the pence; the pounds will take care of themselves.
Economy is too late at the bottom of the purse.
Economy is the wealth of the poor and the wisdom of the rich.

EDUCATION:
A child is better unborn than untaught.
Better untaught than ill-taught.
Education is the poor man's haven (Latin).
Education makes the man.
He that brings up his son to nothing, breeds a thief.
The common school is the greatest discovery ever made by man.
The only really educated men are self-educated.
What sculpture is to a block of marble, education is to the soul.
Public instruction should be the first object of government (Napoleon).
Educated men are as much superior to the uneducated as the living are to the dead.
It is only the ignorant who despise education.
Education is for men and women alike.
Seek education, even in China.
Only the educated are free.

EGG:
Eggs and oaths are most easily broken.

It is very hard to shave an egg.
Omelets are not made without breaking eggs.
ELOQUENCE:
Deluge of words and a drop of sense.
He that has not silver in his purse, should have silver on his tongue.
A flow of words and not a drop of wisdom.
EMPTY:
An empty sack cannot stand upright.
END:
In my end is my beginning (Mary Stuart).
ENDEAVOR:
He that will conquer must fight.
He that will eat the kernel must crack the nut.
    No endeavor is in vain,
        its reward is in the doing.
    And the rapture of pursuing
        is the prize the vanquished gain.
ENDINGS:
All is well that ends well.
Look at the end.
In the end things will mend.
ENDURANCE:
A baited cat may grow as fierce as a lion.
A man may provoke his own dog to bite him.
ENDURE:
He that shall endure unto the end, the same shall be saved (Matt.).
He that endures is not overcome.
What can't be cured were best endured.
ENEMY:
Love your enemy for they tell your faults (Franklin).
If your enemy is hungry give him bread to eat (Prov.).
If we are bound to forgive an enemy, we are not bound to trust him.
A man's greatness can be measured by his enemy.
Once an enemy always an enemy.
Your enemy makes you wise.
Be your enemy an ant see in him an elephant.
An enemy does not sleep.
One enemy is too much.
Rejoice not over the greatest enemy being dead (Apocrypha).

Every wise man dreadeth his enemy.
Though thy enemy be a mouse, yet watch him like a lion.
None but myself ever did me any harm (*Napoleon*).
One foe is too many, and a hundred friends too few.
Even from a foe, a man may learn wisdom.
Better a good enemy than a bad friend.
I would rather my enemies envy me than I envy them.
Man is his own worst enemy.
Enemy charging my fame is an asset. Stones are thrown only against a fruitful branch.

ENOUGH:
Enough is better than too much.

ENVY:
It is better to be envied than pitied.
Expect not praise without envy until you are dead.
As rust corrupts iron, so envy corrupts men.
I would rather my enemies envy me than I envy them.
Envy never enriched a man.

EQUALITY:
Equality begins in the grave.
We are all born equal, and distinguished alone by virtue.
Equal right for all, special privileges for none (*Jefferson*).
We hold these truths to be self-evident, that all men are created equal (*Jefferson*).

ERROR:
The wisest make mistakes.
Erring is not cheating.
I would rather err with Plato than to perceive the truth with others (*Cicero*).
Error is always in haste.
By ignorance we make mistakes, and by mistakes we learn.

EVIL:
Recompense to no man evil for evil (*Rom.*).
Of evil grain good seed can come.
One evil rises out of another.
Evil often triumphs but never conquers.
An evil life is a kind of death.
An evil lesson is soon learned.
Avoid evil and it will avoid thee.

EXAMPLE:
A good example is the best sermon.
They do more harm by their evil example than by their actual sin.

EXCESS:
Every excess becomes a vice.

EXCUSE:
Make excuses for another, never for yourself.
He who excuses himself, accuses himself.

EXPENSE:
Beware of little expense; a small leak will sink a great ship (*Franklin*).

EXPERIENCE:
Experience is the mother of knowledge.
Experience passes science.
He that has been bitten by a serpent is afraid of a rope.

EYE:
If thine eye offend thee, pluck it out and cast it from thee (*Matt.*).
The eye is the mirror of the soul.
Out of the eye, out of the heart.
The eye is the pearl of the face.
The eye is not satisfied with seeing.
The eye lets in love.
The heart's letter is read in the eyes.
The ear is less trustworthy than the eye.
The light of the body is the eye (*Matt.*).
An evil eye can see no good.

F

FACE:
In the faces of men and women I see God (*Whitman*).
Where the face is fair there needs no color.
A fair face is half a fortune.
Man is read in his face.
Men's faces are not to be trusted.
Everyone is satisfied with his own face.
Your face betrays your years.
An ugly face should not curse the mirror.

FACTS:
Facts are stubborn things.
Facts are sharp edges.

FAILURE:
> Failure teaches success.
> He who never fails will never grow rich.

FAIR:
> A honey tongue is a heart of gall.
> Bees that have honey in their mouth have stings in their tails.
> Fair words and wicked deeds deceive wise men and fools.
> Honey catches more flies than vinegar.

FAITH:
> Be thou faithful unto death (Rom.).
> Faith without works is dead (James).
> When the ox falls everybody sharpens his knife.
> The just shall live by faith (Paul).
> We walk by faith not by sight (II Cor.).
> I know that my Redeemer liveth (Job).
> What is faith unless it is to believe what you do not see (St. Augustine).

FALL:
> When a tree is falling every one cries "down with it."
> He that falls by himself never cries.
> All things that rise will fall.
> He that falls today may rise tomorrow.

FAME:
> Fame is the perfume of heroic deeds.
> Fame is but wind.
> Fame is a magnifying glass.
> What is fame compared to happiness.
> Fame is like a river; is narrowest at its source, and broadest afar off.
> Fame like men will grow white as it grows old.
> All fame is dangerous, good brings envy, bad, shame.
> True fame is never the gift of chance (Greek).

FAMINE:
> More die by food than famine.
> All is good in a famine.

FARMING:
> He that by the plough would thrive, himself must either hold or drive.

FASHION:
> The fashion of this world passeth away.

FATE:
   An ass that kicks against the wall received the blow himself.
   Struggle not against the stream.

FATHER:
   A wise son maketh a glad father (Prov.).
   Honor your father and mother to increase your days on the earth.
   It is not a father's anger but silence that a son dreads.
   He that loves the tree loves the branch.
   Like father like son.
   One father can support ten children, but ten children hardly one father.
   One father is more than a hundred school masters.

FAULTS:
   He is lifeless that is faultless.
   A good garden may have good weeds.
   A fault once denied is twice committed.
   By others' faults wise men correct their own.
   Every man has his faults.
   Love your enemies for they tell your faults (Franklin).
   Forget others' faults; remember yours.
   He that commits a fault thinks every one speaks of it.
   Tell me your faults and mend your own.
   One man's fault is another man's lesson.
   The best cloth may have a moth in it.
   We easily forget our faults when nobody knows them.
   We confess our faults in plural and deny them in the singular.
   A fault confessed is half redressed.
   Faults done by night will blush by day.
   The greatest fault is to be conscious of none.
   He that is afraid of wounds must not come nigh a battle.
   Those who live in glass houses should not throw stones at others.
   The fault of another is a good teacher.
   Love him who tells you your faults in practice.
   We see only the faults of others.
   He who wants a mile without fault must walk on foot.

FAVOUR:
   Never remember the benefit conferred nor forget the favour received.
   Grace will last, favour will blast.

FEAR:
   Fear God and your enemies will fear you.
   Fear is the father of courage, and the mother of safety.

Fear kills more than disease.
He that is afraid of wounds, must not come near a battle.
Fear makes men ready to believe the worst.
Fear keeps the garden better than the gardener.
There is no medicine for fear.
Whom they fear they hate.
He that fears leaves let him not go into the woods.
Fear makes the lion tame.
If you are terrible to any beware of many.
He that is bitten by a snake is afraid of a rope.
All fearlessness is folly.
Even the bravest are frightened by sudden terror.
Fear him who fears thee, though he be a fly, and thou an elephant.
A scalded cat fears cold water.
Fear is the beginning of wisdom.
Never lose honour through fear.

FEAST:
Be not made a beggar by banqueting upon borrowing (Apoc.).
Better fare hard with good men, than feast with bad.
Feasting is the physicians' harvest.
Fools make the banquets and wise men enjoy them.
Little difference between a feast and a bellyful.

FEATHER:
Fine feathers make fine birds.
Feather by feather birds build nests.

FEET:
Dry feet, warm head bring safe to bed.

FIDELITY:
Be thou faithful unto the end (Prov.).
It is better to be faithful than famous.
Fidelity gained by bribes is overcome by bribes.

FINGER:
All the fingers are not alike.

FIRE:
Fire and water are good servants but bad masters.
Don't play with fire.

FIRST:
First come, first served.
Better first in a village, than second in Rome.
The first blow is half the battle.

FISH:
    The great fish eat up the small.
    Like a fish out of water.

FIT:
    Every shoe fits not every foot.

FLATTERY:
    A flatterer's mouth worketh ruin (*Apoc.*).
    Better flatter a fool than fight him.
    The Lord shall cut off all flattering lips (*Ps.*).
    Flattery corrupts both the receiver and the giver.
    When flatterers meet the devil goes to dinner.
    Flatterers look like friends, as wolves resemble dogs.
    Flattery is like Eau de Cologne—to be smelt but not swallowed.
    He that hath no honey in his pot, let him have it in his mouth.
    He that loveth the flattered is worthy of the flatterers (*Shakespeare*).
    The same man cannot be friend and flatterer.
    Every flatterer lives at the expense of the person who listens to him (*La Fontaine*).
    A flatterer is a secret enemy.
    One catches more flies with a spoonful of honey than with 20 pounds of vinegar.

FLEA:
    That's a valiant flea who dares eat his breakfast on the lips of a lion (*Shakespeare*).
    Better the wolves eat us than the fleas.

FLESH:
    The spirit indeed is willing, but the flesh is weak (*Matt.*).

FLOWER:
    Even the tiniest flower shall recall the splendour of the world.
    One flower makes no garland.

FLY:
    Flies come to feast uninvited.
    A shut mouth catches no flies.

FOLLOW:
    Follow any river and you will get to the sea.

FOLLY:
    Happy is the man who knows his follies in his youth.
    Folly grows without watering.
    It is a great part of wisdom to find out one's own folly.
    No folly like being in love.

The folly of one man is the fortune of another.
It is folly to lay out money in the purchase of reputation.
FOOL:
A fool's mouth is his destruction (Prov.).
A whip for the horse, bridle for the ass, and a rod for the fool's back (Prov.).
Even a fool, when he holdeth his peace, is counted wise (Prov.).
Fools die for the want of wisdom (Prov.).
It is better to hear the rebuke of the wise, than the song of fools (Prov.).
Let a bear robbed of her cubs meet a man, rather than a fool in his folly (Prov.).
The wise man's eyes are in his head, but the fool walketh in darkness (Eccl.).
A fool is like other men as long as he is silent.
A fool of forty is a fool indeed.
A fool may ask more questions in an hour than a wise man can answer in seven years.
A fool may throw a stone into a well which a hundred wise men cannot pull out.
A fool's paradise is a wise man's hell.
A fool's tongue is long enough to cut his own throat (Shakespeare).
A rich fool is a wise man's treasure.
As the bell clinks, so the fool thinks.
Fools bite one another, but wise men agree together.
Fools tie knots and wise men loose them.
It is better to be a beggar than a fool.
The fool wanders, the wise men travel.
The wise man draws more advantage from his enemies than the fool from his friends (Franklin).
He is a fool who makes his doctor his heir.
With fools it is always holiday.
Better a slap from a wise man, than a kiss from a fool.
When a fool is sent to the market, the store keepers rejoice.
FOOT:
Better a bare foot than none.
The belly warm, the foot sleepy.
FORGE:
You may lead a horse to water, but you can't make him drink.
Force is not a remedy.
You may force a man to shut his eyes, but you can't make him sleep.

FORGET:
    Men are men; the best sometimes forget (*Shakespeare*).

FORGIVE:
    Good to forgive, best to forget (*Browning*).
    Only the brave know how to forgive.
    Forgiveness is better than revenge.

FORTUNE:
    It is better to be born lucky than rich.
    Fortune to one is mother, to another stepmother.
    Every man is the architect of his own actions.
    Fortune and misfortune are neighbors.
    You used to be a baker though now you wear gloves.
    Fortune knocks once at least at every man's gate.
    Good fortune is not known until it is lost.
    He fell today, I may fall tomorrow.
    Where fortune knocks, open the door.
    Fortune is not far from the brave man's head.

FOX:
    If you deal with a fox think of his tricks.
    The old fox need not to be taught tricks.
    The fox said the grapes are sour.
    The fox changes his fur but not his habits.

FREEDOM:
    The sweetest freedom is an honest hand.
    Better be a free bird than a captured king.
    He who has lost freedom has nothing else to lose.
    No bad man is free.
    If the Lord sets you free, you shall be free indeed.
    No man is free who is not master of himself.

FRIEND:
    One God, one wife, but many friends.
    Choose thy friends like thy books, few but choice.
    A faithful friend is the medicine of life.
    Faithful are the wounds of a friend, but the kisses of an enemy are deceitful (*Prov.*).
    Greater love hath no man than this, that a man lay down his life for his friends (*Job*).
    A friend in need is a friend indeed.
    A friend in the market is better than money in the chest.
    A friend is a person with whom I may be sincere (*Emerson*).
    A friend is never known till he is needed.

A friend should bear his friends' infirmities (*Shakespeare*).
The wretches have no friends.
A good friend is my nearest relation.
A man dies as often as he loses his friends (*Bacon*).
Be slow in choosing a friend, slower in changing.
Better an open enemy than a false friend.
Better to abide a friend's anger than a foe's kisses.
Do good to thy friend to keep him, to thy enemy to gain him (*Franklin*).
Friends are as dangerous as enemies.
They are rich who have true friends.
He is a good friend that speaks well of me behind my back.
When fortune begins to frown, friends will be few.
He is my friend that grindeth at my mill.
He will never have true friends who is afraid of making enemies.
I will be thy friend, but not thy vice's friend.
My son, keep well thy tongue, and keep thy friend (*Chaucer*).
Treat your friend as if he might become an enemy.
Old friends are best.
One enemy can do more hurt than ten friends can do good.
The best mirror is an old friend.
The vanquished have no friends.
The wicked have no friends.
Three faithful friends, an old dog, an old wife, and ready money.
Be a friend to yourself and others will befriend you.
Change your pleasures but not your friends.
Nothing is so dangerous as an ignorant friend.
The friends of my friends are my friends.
A false friend has money in his mouth, gall in his heart.
A friend to all is a friend to none.
If you never tell your secret to a friend, you will never fear him, when he becomes your enemy.
We should behave to our friends as we would wish our friends to behave with us.
Before you make a friend eat a bushel of salt with him.
He does good to himself who does good to friends.
Nothing can be purchased which is better than a true friend.
Treat your friend as if he might become an enemy.
Where there are friends there is wealth.
He who has a thousand friends has not a friend to spare.
A courageous foe is better than a cowardly friend.

A father is a treasure, a brother a comfort, but a friend is both.
A faithful friend is the medicine of life.
Three are most excellent, old wine, old gold, and old friend.

FRIENDSHIP:
Friendship is not to be bought at a fare.
While the pot boils, friendship blooms.
Just as yellow gold is tested in the fire, so is friendship tested in adversity (Ovid).

FROG:
The frog's own croak betrays him.
Even a frog would bite if it has teeth.

FRUIT:
Forbidden fruit is sweetest.
Fruit out of season, sorrow out of reason.
He that will have the fruit must climb the tree.
Like tree, like fruit.
It is only at the tree loaded with fruit that people throw stones.

FUNERAL:
After a funeral, a feast.

FUTURE:
Count not too much upon time to come.
Borrow not too much upon time to come.
Have no care for the future, and you will sorrow for the present.
He must be mad who builds upon the future.

G

GAIN:
Gain gotten by a lie will burn one's finger.
Rather lose honorably than gain basely.
No pains, no gains.
Honour and profit lie not all in one sack.
Pain is forgotten when gain comes.
Soon gotten, soon spent.

GAMBLING:
A pack of cards is the devil's prayer-book.
Young gamblers, old beggars.
Gambling is the mother of lies and purgeries.

GARDEN:
As is the garden such is the gardener.

GARDENING:
    He that plants trees loves others besides himself.
    Large trees give more shade than fruit.
GENIUS:
    Genius with education is like silver with gold.
    The first and last thing required of genius is love of truth (*Goethe*).
    When genius is punished its fame is exalted (*Tacitus*).
    Adversity reveals genius, prosperity hides it (*Horace*).
GENTLE:
    A gentle hand may lead the elephant with a hair.
GENTLEMEN:
    He is gentle that doth gentle deeds.
    Manners and money make the gentleman.
GIFT:
    A gift is a precious stone in the eyes of him that hath it.
    A gift blindeth the eyes.
    Secret gifts are openly rewarded.
    Gifts make beggars bold.
    Great gifts are for great men.
    Look not a gift horse in his mouth.
    Rich gifts wax poor when givers prove unkind (*Shakespeare*).
    A gift in the hand is better than two promises.
    Gifts make the water to run back.
    Whatever a man has is only a gift.
    A gift though small is welcome.
    The gifts of a foe are not gifts.
    Beware of him who makes thee presents.
    What is about is cheaper than a gift.
    A man's gift makes room for him.
    He that bringeth a present findeth the door open.
GIRL:
    A girl unemployed is thinking of mischief (*Ovid*).
    Dear to the heart of girls is their own beauty.
GIVING:
    Give and spend, and God will send.
    Some men give of their means, and others of their meanness.
    The hand that gives gathers.
    Give to the poor, and thou shalt have treasure in heaven (*Matt.*).
    God loveth a cheerful giver (*II Cor.*).
    It is more blessed to give than to receive (*Acts*).

Giving much to the poor doth enrich a man's store.
What we gave, we have; what we spent we had; what we left we lost.
To give is the business of the rich (*Goethe*).
To give is honor, to lose is grief.

GLASS:
Whose home is of glass must not throw stones at another's.

GLORY:
"Thus passes the glory of the world" (*Latin*).
No flowery road leads to glory.
We rise in glory as we sink in pride.
Hasty glory goes out in a snuff.

GLUTTONY:
Hunger and thirst scarcely kill any, but gluttony and drink a great many.
I saw few die of hunger; of eating, a hundred thousand.
The table robs more thn a thief.
They have digged their grave with their teeth.
Gluttony kills more than the sword.

GOD:
God is love, and he that dwelleth in love dwelleth in God, and God in him (*John*).
Better God than gold.
God is our refuge and our strength (*Ps.*).
God will provide (*Gen.*).
If God be for us, who can be against us (*Rom.*).
The Lord is my light and my salvation.
Give and spend, and God will send.
Whom the Lord loveth he chasteneth.
Be careful to whom you give.
Father and mother are kind but God is kinder.
God does not pay weekly, but he pays in the end.
God helps them who help themselves.
In the faces of men and women I see God (*Whitman*).
Just are the ways of God and justifiable to man (*Milton*).
Where there is peace God is.
To be is to live with God.
Have God and have all.
God often visits us, but most of the time we are not at home.
If God did not exist, it would be necessary to invent him (*Voltaire*).

What God will, no frost can kill.
He is to be feared who fears not God.
God has given and God has taken away.
God knows what He does.
God punishes with one hand and blesses with the other.

GOLD:
Gold is proved by touch.
The balance distinguishes not between gold and lead.
Gold had been the ruin of many (Apoc.).
A golden dart kills while it pleases.
A golden hammer breaks an iron gate.
All is not gold that glitters.
Chains of gold are stronger than the chains of iron.
Gold dust blinds all eyes.
Gold gives in at any gate, except of heaven's.
A man of straw is worth a woman of gold.
Gold is a good doctor.
Gold maketh an honest man an ill man.
Gold is an unseen tyrant.
Gold opens all locks.
Gold were as good as twenty orators (Shakespeare).
What words won't do gold will.
Gold shines in the mud.

GOLDEN RULE:
Whatsoever ye would that men should do unto you, do ye even so to them (Matt.).

GOOD:
All good comes to end except the goodness of God.
Good finds good.
Good that comes too late is good as nothing.
Abhor that which is evil, cleave to that which is good.

GOODNESS:
Let us not be weary in well doing (Gal.).
True goodness springs from a man's own heart.
Be good if you expect to receive it.
The evil that men do lives after them.
If you wish to be good, first believe that you are bad (La Rouchefoucauld).
The good man makes others good.
To a good man nothing that happens is evil.
For ill do well, then fear not hell.

He that returns a good for evil obtains the victory.
A good fellow is a costly name.
A good man can do no more harm than a sheep.

GOSSIPS:
A gossip speaks ill of all and of her.
Gossips are frogs, they drink and talk.
Gossipping and lying go together.

GOVERNMENT:
The whole of government consists in the art of being honest (*Jefferson*).
They would govern the most make the least voice.
A wise man neither suffers himself to be governed, nor attempts to govern others (*Le Bruyère*).

GRACE:
Grace will last, favour will blast.

GRADUAL:
Feather by feather the goose is plucked.
Step by step the ladder's ascended.

GRAPES:
When the fox cannot reach the grapes, he says they are not ripe.

GRASS:
Grass grows at last above all graves.

GRATITUDE:
Cast no dirt into the well that gives you water.
The river past and God forgotten.
To a grateful man give money when he needs.
We must not speak ill of the bridge that carries us safe over.
Gratitude is the least of virtues, ingratitude the worst of vices.
Do not cut down the tree that gives you shade.
In every thing give thanks (*I Thess.*).
To the grateful man give more than he asks.
Gratitude makes graces everlasting.

GRAVE:
Six feet of grave makes all equal.
The churchyard graves are of all sizes.
The grave is the general meeting place.
All our pomp the earth covers.
We shall all lie alike in our graves.
Only in the grave is there rest.
There the wicked cease from troubling, and there the weary be at rest (*Job*).

GREAT:
>   A great ship asks deep waters.
>   An eagle does not catch flies.
>   Great men are not always wise.
>   Great hopes make the great man.
>   Great men have more adorers than friends.
>   Great men are often overthrown by small means.
>   Great without small make a bad wall.
>   The greatest men are the simplest.
>   He is great whose faults can be numbered.
>   Great men's sons seldom do well.
>   It is a rough road that leads to the height of greatness.

GREED:
>   A greedy man God hates.
>   Greedy folks have long arms.

GRIEF:
>   Grief should be the instruction of the wise (*Byron*).
>   The only cure for grief is action.
>   Grief is a "species" of idleness.
>   Patience is the best remedy for grief.
>   Grief makes an hour two.
>   Great souls suffer in silence (*Schiller*).

GRUMBLING:
>   Grumbling makes the load no larger.

GUARD:
>   Guard yourself not only against your enemies but also your friends.

GUEST:
>   A constant guest is never welcome.
>   First and new guests swell in three days.
>   Uninvited guests sit on thorns.

GUILT:
>   Suspicion always haunts the guilty mind (*Shakespeare*).
>   He who is guilty believes all men speak ill of him.
>   Guilt is always jealous.
>   He that knows no guilt can know no fear.
>   Men that are greatly guilty are never wise.

H

HABIT:
>   Habit is overcome by habit.
>   Habit is stronger than nature.

Habit is second nature (*Montaigne*).
Habit is ten times nature.
How many unjust things are done from habit.

HAIR:
The very hairs of your head are numbered.
Short hair is soon brushed.
Hair adds beauty to a good face, and terror to an ugly one.
Ugly is a field without grass, a plant without leaves, or a head without hair (*Ovid*).
It is not the white hair that engenders wisdom.
Gray hairs are death's blossoms.

HALF:
Half a loaf is better than no bread.
Never do things by halves.

HAND:
A clean hand wants no washing.
A cold hand a warm heart.
Nothing enters into a closed hand.
Kiss the hand which you cannot bite.
Worse than a bloody hand is a hard heart.
A clean glove often hides a dirty hand.
Let not your left hand know what the right hand gives away.
Hands were made for honest labor, not to plunder or to steal.
A wise hand will make tools of what comes to hand.
The right hand is slave to the left.
God looks with favor at pure, not full, hands.

HANDSOME:
A handsome shoe often pinches the foot.
A handsome flower is not sweetest.

HANGING:
We must all hang together or we shall all hang separately (*Franklin*).

HAPPEN:
What happens to one may happen to another.
Everybody is wise after the thing has happened.
What does not happen in a year may happen in a moment.

HAPPINESS:
Better be happy than wise.
Happiness is a habit to be cultivated.
Happy the man who aims through all his life to lessen hatred and diminish strife.

    No happiness without holiness.
    Call no man happy till he dies.
    Happiness just whistles past the pessimist.
    Happiness is but a name.
    Happiness of men consists in life, and life is in labor (*Tolstoy*).
    Man is not born for happiness.
    Happiness does away with ugliness.
    A happy life consists in tranquility of mind.
HARE:
    Hares are not caught with drums.
HARM:
    It costs more to do ill than to do well.
HARVEST:
    He that has a good harvest may be content with some thistles.
HASTE:
    Haste makes waste.
    Haste and wisdom are things far different.
    Haste is of the devil.
    Hasty people will never make good midwives.
    Nothing is more vulgar than haste.
HAT:
    Pull down your hat on the windy side.
HATE:
    A true man hates none.
    Hatred is blind, as well as love.
    Hating people is burning down your own house to get rid of a rat (*Forsduck*).
    Let them hate me so long as they fear me.
    Hatred is the coward's revenge for being intimidated (*G. B. Shaw*).
    In time we hate that which we often fear (*Shakespeare*).
HAVE:
    If you have not what you like, you must like what you have.
HEAD:
    Two heads are better than one.
    He that hath a head of wax must not walk in the sun.
    Better be the head of an ass than the tail of a horse.
    One good head is better than a thousand hands.
    He that has a head of glass must not throw stones at another.
HEALTH:
    Health is not valued till sickness comes.

Good wife and health is man's best wealth.
After dinner sit a while, after supper walk a mile.
Health is better than meat.
Health is great riches.
The first wealth is health (*Emerson*).
Diet cures more than doctors.
The best doctors in the world are Doctor Diet, Doctor Quiet, and Dr. Merryman.
Joy and temperance and repose slam the door in the doctor's nose (*Longfellow*).
Early to bed, and early to rise, makes a man healthy, wealthy and wise.
An apple a day keeps the doctor away.
Head and feet keep warm, the rest will take no harm.
A sound mind in a sound body.
He that goes to bed thirsty rises healthy.
Guard the health both of body and of soul.
He who has good health is young.
He destroys his health by labouring to preserve it.
To the well man every day is a feast.

HEAR:
Hear twice before you speak once.
From hearing comes wisdom, from speaking repentance.
Hear both sides.
Hear first and speak afterwards.

HEART:
Out of the abundance of the heart, the mouth speaketh (*Matt.*).
Where your treasure is, there will your heart be also (*Luke*).
A gentle heart is tied with an easy thread.
A good heart cannot lie.
A good heart conquers all fortunes.
Kind hearts are more than coronets (*Tennyson*).
Knit your heart with an unslipping heart (*Shakespeare*).
What the heart did think, the heart would clink.
When the heart is on fire, some sparks fly out of the mouth.
Where hearts are true, few words will do.
The heart is deceitful above all things, and desperately wicked.
Every one speaks well of his heart, but no one dares speak ill of the head.
A generous heart repairs a slanderous tongue (*Homer*).
The heart of the fool is in his mouth, but the mouth of the wise, is in his heart.

    A wounded heart is hard to cure.
    A happy heart is better than a full purse.
    A good heart helps in misfortunes.
HEAVEN:
    Better go to heaven in rags, than to hell in embroidery.
    Heaven helps those who help themselves.
    He that would conquer heaven must fight.
    No man must go to heaven, who hath not sent his heart thither before.
    No man can resolve himself into heaven (*Moody*).
    Heaven without good souls cannot be heaven.
    Heaven's never deaf but when man's heart is dumb. (*Quarter*).
    He who offends himself against Heaven has none to whom he can pay (*Confucius*).
    Even the hen when it drinks water looks toward heaven.
HEAVY:
    Every horse thinks his pack heavy.
HEDGE:
    Hedges have eyes and wells have ears.
    A low hedge is easily leaped over.
HEIR:
    The third heir settleth all over.
    The grief of the heir is only masked laughter.
HELL:
    Hell is wherever heaven is not.
    Hell and chancellery are all always open.
    For ill do well, then fear no hell.
    Hell is the wrath of God, His hate of sin.
    The descent to hell is easy.
HELP:
    Every little helps.
    Though one grain fills not the sack, it helps.
    Help is good everywhere except at one's dinner.
    Vain is the help of man.
    God helps them that help themselves.
    Slow help is no help.
    Even the just have need of help.
    It is a kindly act to help the fallen.
HEN:
    It is a bad hen that eats at your house and lays at another.
    A black hen will lay a white egg.

HEROES:
    It is fortune chiefly that makes heroes.
    Hero worship is stronger where there is at least regard for human freedom.
    A hero is only known in time of misfortune.
    One brave deed makes no hero.
    To be conquered by a hero is an honor.
    A man must be a hero to understand a hero.
    There are heroes in evil as well as in good.
    The hero is known on the battlefield.

HESITATE:
    The woman who hesitates is lost.

HIDING:
    Hiders are good finders.

HIGH:
    The highest tree has the greatest fall.
    High houses are mostly empty in the upper storey.

HILL:
    There is no hill without a valley.

HISTORY:
    History repeats itself.
    Happy is the nation that has no history.
    History is lies agreed upon.
    Sin writes histories' goodness in silence (Goethe).

HOLE:
    The hole calls the thief.

HOLIDAY:
    A perpetual holiday is a good working definition of hell (G. B. Shaw).
    It is not a holiday that it is not kept holy.

HOME:
    Be grateful at home.
    In the nest is a throat for song, as well as a beak for food.
    Dry bread at home is better than roast meat abroad.
    East or West, home is best.
    Every bird likes its own nest.
    Every dog is a lion at home.
    Men make houses, women make homes.
    The smoke of a man's own house is better than the fire of another.
    There is no place like home.
    Be not a lion in thy house, nor frantic among the servants (Apoc.).

He that is far from home is near to harm.
A little house well filled, a little land well tilled and a little wife well willed.
To be happy at home is the ultimate result of all ambition.
A man without a home is a bird without a nest.
Be it ever so humble, there is no place like home (*Payne*).
Home is where the heart is.
Where the nest and eggs are, the birds are near.
Whom God loves, his home is sweet to him.
Who is happy should hide at home.
He that has no rest at home is in the world's hell.

HONESTY:
Honest men fear neither the light nor the dark.
Honesty is the best policy.
An honest man does not make himself a dog for the sake of a bone.
An honest man is not the worse because a dog barks at him.
An honest man is the noblest work of God.
He that is wise is honest.
He that loses his honesty has nothing else to lose.
No legacy so rich as honesty (*Shakespeare*).
The measure of life is not length, but honesty.
A clean mouth and an honest hand.
Clean hands are better than full ones.

HONEY:
A drop of honey catches more flies than a barrel of vinegar.
When you test honey remember gall.
Make yourself all honey and the flies will devour you.
He who would gather honey must bear the sting of bees.

HONOUR:
The king may give honour, but you must make yourself honorable.
Where honor ceaseth, there knowledge decreaseth.
Honor without profit is a ring on the finger.
Honor thy father and thy mother.
Honor the tree that gives you shelter.
He that desires honor, is not worthy of honor.
He that hath no honor had no sorrow.
Honor shows the man.
Honor is but an empty bubble.
If I lose mine honor, I lose myself (*Shakespeare*).
Take honour from me and my life is done (*Shakespeare*).

The louder he talketh of his honor, the further we counted our spoons.

When faith is lost, when honor dies, the man is dead (*Whitman*).

All is lost save honour.

Without money honor is nothing but a malady.

Let me do what honour demands.

It is no honor for an eagle to vanquish a dove.

Don't run after honors, and they will come to you by themselves.

HOPE:

Great hopes make great men.

As long as there is life there is hope.

Hope is the poor man's income.

Who lives by hope will die of hunger.

Take hope from man and you make him a beast.

The miserable has no medicines, but only hope (*Shakespeare*).

Hope to the end (*Peter*).

A man may hope for any thing while he has life.

HORSE:

Judge not the horse by his saddle.

When the manger is empty the horses fight.

One whip is enough for a good horse, and a bad one not a thousand.

A groaning horse, and a groaning wife, never fail their master.

HOSPITALITY:

Be not forgetful to entertain strangers, for thereby some have entertained angels unawares.

The first day a man is a guest, the second a burden, the third a pest.

HOT TEMPERS:

When the head is hot, the hand is ready.

HOUR:

For the unhappy how slowly pass the hours.

An hour in the morning before breakfast is worth like all the rest of the day.

Pleasure and action make the hours seem short.

Hours were made for man, and not man for the hours.

Sweetest hours fly fastest.

The hour which gives us life begins to take it away.

HOUSE:

It is a sad house where the hen crows louder than the cock.

A house divided against itself cannot stand.

HOUSEKEEPER:
> Everything is of use to a housekeeper.

HUMANITY:
> Be ashamed to die until you have won some victory for humanity (Horace Mann).

HUMILITY:
> Whosoever shall smite thee on the right cheek, turn him the other also (Matt.).
> Whosoever exalteth himself shall be abased, and he that humbleth himself shall be exalted (Luke).
> There is no true holiness without humility.
> Humility often gains more than pride.
> Too much humility is pride.
> He that knows himself best, esteems himself least.
> Make yourself a lamb and the wolf will eat you.
> He that is humble ever shall have God to be his Guide (Bunyan).
> Humility is the foundation of all virtue.
> Humble thy self in all things.

HUMOUR:
> Humor is gravity concealed behind a jest.

HUNGER:
> A hungry man is an angry man.
> A hungry man smells meat after off.
> A hungry dog does not fear the stick.
> Hunger and cold delivers a man up to his enemy.
> Hunger fetches the wolf out of the woods.
> Hunger is sharper than the sword.
> Hunger finds no fault with the cook.
> Hunger knows no friend.
> The full belly does not believe in hunger.
> Hunger changes beans into almonds.
> They that die by famine die by inches.
> A hungry stomach, an angry face.
> An angry face indicates a hungry stomach.

HUNTING:
> Hunting, hawking, and love for one joy have a hundred griefs.
> Don't think to hunt two hares with one dog.

HUSBAND:
> Husbands, love your wives, and be not bitter against them (Coloss.).
> A good husband makes a good wife.

A good wife makes a good husband.
To know the husband observe the face of the wife.
A wedded man lives in sorrow and care.
A happy couple, the husband deaf, the wife blind.
Emperors are only husbands in wife's eyes (*Byron*).
A husband with one eye rather than one son.
In the husband wisdom, in the wife gentleness.
Husbands are in heaven whose wives scold not.
The calmest husbands make the stormiest wives.
When the husband dies the neighbors learn how many children he has.
Serve your husband as a master, beware of him as a traitor (*Montaigne*).

HYPOCRISY:
Hypocrisy can find a cloak for rain.
A mouth that prays and a hand that kills.
Ye blind guides, which strain at a gnat and swallow a camel (*Matt.*).
Woe unto, ye scribes and pharisees, hypocrites, for ye are like white sepulchres (*Matt.*).
The devil can cite Scriptures for his purposes.
The cat shuts its eyes when stealing the cream.
He carries fire in one hand and water in the other.
I hate a bad man saying what is good.

I

ICE:
Trust not to one night the ice, when it cracks to bears; when it bends, it breaks.

IDEA:
Wise men possess ideas; most of us are possessed by them.

IDLENESS:
An empty skull is the devil's workshop.
An idle person is the devil's play fellow.
Be not idle and you shall not be longing.
By doing nothing we learn to do ill.
Idle dogs worry sheep.
Idleness is the greatest prodigality in the world.
Idleness is the key of beggary.
If the brain sows not corns it plants thistles.
If the devil catch a man idle he will send him to work.

In the evening the idle man begins to be busy.
No man shall live in the world that has nothing to do in it.
Standing pools gather filth.
The dead only should do nothing.
Of idleness comes no goodness.
Go to the ant, thou sluggard; consider her ways and be wise (*Prov.*).
He who does nothing but sit and eat will wear away a mountain of wealth.
The tongue of idle persons is never idle.
When we do ill the devil tempteth us; when we do nothing we tempt him.
The idle mind knows not what it wants.
Expect poison from the standing water (*Blake*).
Idleness is the nurse of vices.
To do nothing is in every man's power.
Idleness is a sepulchre of living man.

IGNORANCE:
He that knows nothing doubts nothing.
Better unfed than untaught.
A man without knowledge is like one that is dead.
Ignorance never settled a quarrel.
Being ignorant is not so much a shame as being unwilling to learn.
The ignorant has an eagle's wings and an owl's eyes.
Our lives are shortened by our ignorance.
I am not ashamed to confess that I am ignorant of what I do not know (*Cicero*).
Better unborn than untaught.
It is well to be ignorant of many things.

ILL:
Ill doers are ill thinkers.
He who has done ill once will do it again.

ILL GOTTEN:
Ill-got; Ill-spent.

IMAGINATION:
Imagination is the eye of the soul.
Imagination is more important than knowledge.

IMITATION:
Imitation is the sincerest flattery.

There is no difference between imitation and counterfeiting.
By looking at squinting people you learn to squint.

IMMORTALITY:
God created man to be immortal.
All men desire to be immortal.
He hath not lived that lives not after death.
Immortality is the glorious discovery of Christianity (*Channing*).
He sins against this life who slights the next.
There is nothing strictly immortal but immortality.
Belief in the future life is the appetite of reason (*Landor*).

IMPATIENCE:
Rome was not built in a day.
Troy was not taken in a day.
The tree falls not at first stroke.

IMPOSSIBLE:
All things are possible.
You cannot clap with one hand.
Nothing is impossible to a willing beast.
The inverted pyramid will never stand.
You can not sell the cow and have the milk.
"Impossible" . . . that is not French (*Napoleon*).
You cannot drink and whistle at the same time.

IMPRESSION:
First impressions are most lasting.
First impression is the best impression.

INCONSISTENCE:
He leaps into a deep river to avoid a shallow brook.
To jump into the water for fear of the rain.

INCURABLE:
What can't be cured can be endured.

INDECISION:
No man having put his hand to the plough and looking back is fit for the Kingdom of God (*Luke*).
He who considers too much will perform little.
Through indecision opportunity is often lost.
While we consider when to begin, it becomes too late.

INDEPENDENCE:
Independence like honor is a rocky island without a beach (*Napoleon*).
The strongest man in the world is he who stands most alone.

Follow your own bent, no matter what people say.
Every man for himself and God for us all.

INDIVIDUALITY:
Different men have different opinions; some like apples and some like onions.

INDUSTRY:
Where bees are there is honey.
To a boiling pot flies come not.
Diligence is the motto of good fortune.
The sleepy fox catches no poultry.
The used key is always bright.

INFECTION:
One scabbed sheep will taint a whole flock.

INFLUENCE:
Each, in corrupting others, corrupts himself.
A cock has great influence on his own dunghill.
A friend in court is worth a penny in the purse.

INGRATITUDE:
As soon as you have drunk, you turn your back upon the spring.
Ingratitude is the daughter of pride.
Hell is full of ingratitude.
A thankless man never does a thankful deed.
How sharper than a serpent's tooth it is to have a thankless child (Shakespeare).
Save a thief from the gallows and he will cut your throat.
Earth produces nothing worse than an ungrateful man.
The wicked is always ungrateful.

INHERITANCE:
The tears of an heir are laughter under a mask.

INJURY:
It costs more to revenge injuries than to bear them.
Write injuries in sand, benefits in marble.
A worthy man forgets past injuries.
How bitter it is when you have sown benefits to reap injuries.
It is better to receive than do an injury.
He that hurts another hurts himself.
The remedy for injuries is to forget them.
He is the wretch that does the injury, not he that endures it.

INJUSTICE:
To do injustice is more desirable than to suffer it (Plato).

INK:
>One drop of ink may make a million think.

INNOCENCE:
>The innocent are gay.
>Innocence is its own defense.
>He that is innocent may well be confident.

INQUISITIVENESS:
>Enquire not what is in another pot.

INSIGNIFICANT:
>The smallest insect may cause death by its bite.
>The least and weakest man can do some harm.
>A spark may consume a city.

INSPIRATION:
>Ninety percent of inspiration is perspiration.

INSTINCT:
>By a divine instinct men's minds mistrust ensuing danger (*Shakespeare*).

INSULT:
>An injury is much sooner forgiven than an insult.
>It is often better to see an insult than to avenge it.
>Insults are like bad coins, we cannot help their being offered, but we need not take them.

INTELLIGENCE:
>All things are slaves to intelligence.

INTENTION:
>Stain not fair acts with foul intentions (*Browne*).
>Muddy springs will have muddy streams.
>Nothing is invented and perfected at the same time.

INVITATION:
>He who comes uncalled, sits unserved.

IRON:
>Iron long fired becomes steel.
>Iron shapes iron.
>We must beat the iron while it is hot.

IRRETRIEVABLE:
>It is no use crying over spilt milk.

J

JEALOUSY:
>When there is love there is jealousy.
>A jealous woman believes everything her passion suggests.

Jealousy is inborn in women's hearts.
Love is never without jealousy.
A jealous man's horns hang in his eyes.
Jealousy is cruel as the grave.
Jealousy shuts one door and opens two.

JESTS:
A joke never gains an enemy, but often loses a friend.
An ill-timed jest has ruined many.
Better love a jest than a friend.

JOURNEYS:
Make short the miles with talk and smiles.

JOY:
We should publish our joys and conceal our griefs.
God send you joy, for sorrow will come fast enough.
After sorrow joy.
Great joys weep, great sorrows laugh.
Who bathes in worldly joys, swims in a world of fear.
No joy without annoy.
There is not a joy the world can give like that taken away (*Byron*).

JUDGE:
Judge not that ye be not judged (*Matt.*).
Never judge by appearance.
He who is a judge between two friends loses one of them.
When a judge puts on his robe, he puts off any relation to any.
Hear the other side.
The upright judge condemns the crime, but does not hate the criminal.
Thieves for their robbery have authority when judges steal themselves (*Shakespeare*).

JUDGMENT:
Say no ill of the year till it is gone.
Haste in judgment is criminal.
Things present are judged by things past.
Who reproves the lame must go upright.

JUSTICE:
Justice without wisdom is impossible.
Justice is truth in action.
Every place is safe to him who lives in justice.
Extreme justice is often extreme injustice.
Justice is half religion.
You are guilty of a crime when you do not punish crime.

Pardon one offense and you encourage many.
Who spares the bad seeks to corrupt the good.
As soon as justice returns, the golden age returns (Virgil).
We love justice greatly, and just men but little.
Justice is blind.
Live and let live is the will of common justice.

K

KEY:
> The key that is used grows bright.
> Not every key fits every lock.

KIN:
> Affinity in hearts is the nearest kindred.

KINDNESS:
> A forced kindness deserveth no thanks.
> Kindness like grain increases by sowing.
> A word of kindness is better than a stuffed sheep.
> A wise man may be kind without cost.
> Kindness knows repentance.
> Kindness consists in loving people more than they deserve
> Kindness is nobler than revenge.

KING:
> Honour the King (I Peter).
> He is the fountain of honour (Bacon).
> Whoever is king is also the father of his country.

KISS:
> The kisses of an enemy are deceitful.
> A kiss of the mouth often touches not the heart.
> After kissing comes more kindness.
> Kisses are keys.
> Many kiss the hand they wish to cut off.

KNAVES:
> It is merry when knaves meet.
> An old knave is no babe.
> Knaves and fools divide the world.

KNOWLEDGE:
> A man without knowledge is one that is dead.
> A little learning is a dangerous thing.
> Knowledge comes but justice lingers.
> Knowledge is a treasure but practice is the key to it.
> To know is not to know, unless someone else knows that I k

He knows most, that knows he knows little.
He knows much that speaks little.
Those who really thirst for knowledge always get it.
Knowledge is the action of the soul.
He knows enough that knows how to hold his peace.
To know everything is to know nothing.
Who knows most believes least.

L

LABOR:
>In all labor there is profit.
The laborer is worthy of his hire (*Luke*).
The sleep of a laboring man is sweet (*Eccl.*).
A man of many trades, begs his bread on Sundays.
Honest labor bears a lovely face.
Labor as long lived; pray as ever dying.
Labor is the law of happiness.
Labor conquers everything.
Labor is often the father of pleasure.
Virtue proceeds through toils.
A good laborer is better than a bad priest.
Sweet is the memory of past labor.
If I had not lifted up the stone, you had not found the jewel.
To labor is to pray.
He who would eat the kernel, must crack the shell.
Who does not teach his child a trade brings him up to steal.

LAMB:
>Make yourself a lamb and the wolves will eat you.

LAME:
>The lame returns sooner than his servant.

LAMP:
>If you would have your lamp burn, you must pour oil into it.

LAND:
>Who has land has war.
Many a man for land, liveth for shame.

LANGUAGE:
>He who is ignorant of foreign languages knows not his own (*Goethe*).
The knowledge of the ancient languages is mainly a luxury.
Language is the dress of thought.

Speak that I may see you.
Language was the immediate gift of God (*Webster*).

LASS:
He that loves glass without "G."
Take away 1 and that is he.
Glasses and lasses are brittle ware.

LAST:
Last but not least.
The hindmost dog may catch the hare.
The last drop makes the cup run over.
It is the last one whom the dog attack.

LATE:
It is too late to come to the well when the child is drowned.
Better late than never.
It is too late to lock the stable door when the horse is stolen.
He who comes late must eat what is left.

LAUGH:
A good laugh is sunshine in the house.
Laugh and grow fat.
A maid that laughs is half taken.
And if I laugh at any mortal thing, 'tis that I may not weep (*Byron*).
He is not laughed at that laughs at himself first.
He who laughs too much has the nature of a fool.
Laugh and the world laughs with you; weep, and you weep alone (*Wilcox*).
The vulgar often laugh but never smile (*Chesterfield*).
That day is lost on which one has not laughed.
Laughter comes of itself, so does weeping.

LAVISHNESS:
Lavishness is not generosity.

LAW:
He that goes to law holds a wolf by the ears.
God help the sheep when the wolf is judge.
Law makers should not be lawbreakers.
Extreme law, extreme injustice.
Laws too gentle are seldom obeyed; too severe seldom executed (*Franklin*).
When men are pure, laws are written; when men are corrupt laws are broken.
The law is for the protection of the weak more than the strong.

Laws were made to be broken.
Judges should have two ears, both alike.
The man who does no wrong needs no law.
Fear not the law but the judge.

LAWYER:
Few lawyers die well, few physicians live well.
A peasant between two lawyers is like a fish between two cats.
The good have no need of an advocate.
If there were no bad people, there would be no good lawyers.
Lawyers are more ready to get a man into trouble than out of it.
If the laws could speak, they would first complain of lawyers.

LAZINESS:
A lazy sheep thinks its wool heavy.
A lazy boy and a warm bed are difficult to part.
A life of leisure and a life of laziness are two things.
The sleeping fox catches no poultry.
To the lazy every day is a holiday.
He is willing to swallow but too lazy to chew.

LEADER:
He that rides behind another, must not think to guide.
Whoever is foremost leads the herd.

LEAK:
A small leak will sink a ship.

LEAN:
You must take the lean with the fat.

LEAP:
Look before you leap.

LEARN:
Better learn late than never.
Live and learn.
It is lawful to learn even from an enemy.
As the old cock crows so crows the young.

LEARNING:
Learning without thought is labor lost; thought without learning is dangerous.
Learn to live as you would wish to die.
A man becomes learned by asking questions.
He that lives well is learned enough.
I pity unlearned gentlemen on a rainy day.
Learning is the eye of the mind.
Learning makes the wise wiser and the fool more foolish.

Swallow your morning in the morning, digest it in the evening.
A single day among the learned lasts longer than the longest life of the ignorant (Seneca).
A learned man has always wealth in himself.
How many perish in the earth through vain learning.
Much learning shows how much mortals know.
Of what use is learning without understanding.

LEG:
Lose one leg rather than life.

LEISURE:
Leisure is the reward of labor.
Leisure is the time for doing something useful.
Leisure nourishes the body and the mind.
Leisure with dignity.
Leisure without study is death.
You will soon break the bow if you keep it always stretched.

LEND:
It is better to give one shilling than to lend one pound.
Great spenders are bad lenders.
Lend to an enemy and you will gain him; to a friend and you will lose him.
Lend only which you can afford to lose.
What we spent we had, what we have we have, what we lend we lost.
He who lends to the poor gets his interest from God.
Who lends loses double.
You buy yourself an enemy when you lend a man money.
What you lend is lost.
Lent, I was a friend, when asked I was unkind.
Lend to your friend and ask payment of your enemy.

LENITY:
To much lenity makes robbers bold.

LETTERS:
As keys do open chests, so letters open breasts.

LIAR:
Show me a liar and I will show you a thief.
The greater the fool the greater the liar.
Liars begin by imposing on others, and end by deceiving themselves.
A liar is not believed if he speaks the truth.
A liar is sooner caught than the cripple.

A liar needs a good memory.
A liar believes no one.
Liars are always more disposed to swear.

LIBERTY:
Where the spirit of the Lord is, there is liberty (*II Cor.*).
A crust of bread is liberty.
Where liberty dwells there is my country (*Franklin*).
God grants liberty only to those who love it.
It is not good to have too much liberty.
Lean liberty is better than fat slavery.

LIBRARY:
The true university of these days is a collection of books (*Carlyle*).
A group of silent friends.
Food for the soul (*Inscription on library*).

LIE:
Lying lips are an abomination unto the Lord (*Prov.*).
A lie is a coward's way of getting out of trouble.
A lie stands on one leg, truth on two.
Children and fools cannot lie.
Better speak rudely, than lie correctly.
A lie begets a lie till they come to generations.
Half the truth is often a great lie.
He that does not speak truth to me does not believe me as I speak truth.
Old men and far travellers may lie by authority.
No law for lying.
It is better to be lied about than to lie.
Sin has many tools, but a lie is a handle which fits them all (*Holmes*).
A lie never grows old.
Lies have short legs.
From long journeys long lies.
He that has led a wicked life is afraid of his own memories.

LIFE:
Two things doth prolong thy life—a quiet heart and a loving wife.
As for man, his days are as grass (*Prov.*).
Man's life on earth is warfare (*Job.*)
Every man's life is a fairy tale written by God's finger (*Anderson*).
Life is a battle.
A long life may not be good enough, but a good life is long enough.

As a man lives, so shall he die.
As a tree falls so shall he lie.
An ill life, an ill end.
He lives in fame who dies in virtue's cause (Shakespeare).
Look at the end of life.
I wept when I was born and every day shows why.
Life is an empty dream.
Life is a treasure that diminishes daily. What folly to waste it in vain anxieties.
Life is not for time, but for eternity.

LIFE, MAXIMS FOR:
Be just to all, but trust not all.
Be good and refrain not to be good.
The business of life is to go forward.
The web of our life is misled yarn, good and ill together (Shakespeare).
This life is but a thoroughfare full of woe, and we but pilgrims to and fro (Chaucer).
We live and die, but which is best you know no more than I (Byron).
Whilst I yet live, let me not live in vain.
Who lives will see.
A bad life, a bad end.
A useless life is an early death (Goethe).
Do not all you can, spend not all you can, believe not all you hear, and tell not all you know.
As leaves on the trees, is the life of man (Homer).
Choose the best life.
Life is a battle.
Life is not to be bought with heaps of gold.
Live today, forget the past.
Look at the end of life.
Not life itself, but living ill, is evil.
Live and learn.
The art of life is to know how to enjoy a little and endure much.
As long as you live, keep learning how to live.
Keep your purse and your mouth close.
Keep yourself from the anger of a great man, from the tumult of a mob, from a man of ill fame, from a widow that has thrice married, from a wind that comes in at a hole, and from a reconciled enemy.

One God no more, but friends, good store.
He who lives for no one, does not necessarily live for himself.
It is a misery to be born, a pain to live, a trouble to die (St. Bernard).
Life is nearer every day to death.
Life is an empty dream.
Live as if you were to die tomorrow.
Live and let live.
Live righteously, you shall die righteously.
Life consists of what we put into it, not what we find in it.
Live not to eat, but eat to live.
Man has been lent, not given to life.
Life is too short for mean anxieties.
Nature has given man no better than shortness of life.
Oh, life, how long to the wretched, how short to the happy.
He that would live in peace and rest, must hear and see and say the least.
A good life is a garden which yields its brightest colours at noon, and its greatest fragrance at evening.

LIGHT:
Light is sown for the righteous (Ps.).
Walk while you have the light, lest darkness come upon you.
I am the light of the world (John).
Every light has its shadow.
"More light" (Goethe's last words).

LIGHTNING:
When you can use the lightning it is better than cannon (Napoleon).

LIKENESS:
Birds of same feather flock together.
Like pot, like cover.
Like, likes like.
Like cures like.
Like father, like son.

LILY:
Consider the lilies of the field, they toil not, neither do they spin (Matt.).

LION:
It is not good to wake a sleeping lion.
Even a lion must defend himself against the flies.
Be the tail of a lion, rather than the head of a fox.

Even hares pull the lion by the beard when he is dead.
A lion may be beholden to a mouse.
An old lion is better than a young ass.
The lion is not so fierce as they paint him.
The lion's skin is never cheap.
Destroy the lion while he is yet but a whelp.
Who nourishes a lion must obey him.

LIP:
The lips that touch liquor must never touch mine.
Lips are not part of the head, only a door for the mouth.

LISTEN:
To a good listener a few words.
It takes a great man to be a good listener.
Take care of what you say before a well.
A pair of good ears will drain dry a hundred tongues.

LITERATURE:
Literature is a bad crutch but a good walking stick.

LITTLE:
A little pot soon hot.
Little and often fills the purse.
Little strokes fell great oaks.
Of a little take a little and leave a little.
Little drops produce storms.
Little drops produce a shower.
A little house well filled, a little land well tilled, and a little wife well willed.

LOCK:
No lock will hold against the power of gold.
A lock is made only for the honest man, the thief will break it.

LONDON BRIDGE:
London Bridge was made for wise men to go over and fools to go under.

LOOKS:
He that is not handsome at twenty, nor strong at thirty, nor rich at forty, nor wise at fifty, will never be handsome, strong, rich, or wise.
A valiant man's look is more than a coward's sword.
Look before you leap.
The proof of the pudding is in the eating, not its looks.

LOSE:
Better lose the anchor than the whole ship.

What is lost in the fire must be sought in the ashes.
He loseth nothing that loseth not God.
Lose a leg rather than a life.
Loss is no shame.
Praising what is lost makes the remembrance dear (Shakespeare).
The cheerful loser is a winner.
We do not know what is good until we have lost it.

LOVE:
Better a dinner of herbs, where love is, than a stalled ox and hated therewith (Prov.).
Only a wise man knows how to love.
A man has a choice to begin love, but not to tend it.
Love makes a good eye squint.
Absence sharpens love, presence strengthens it.
Love can make any place agreeable.
Hope is live's staff.
Hasty love is soon hot and soon cold.
No herb will cure love.
If you would be loved, love and be lovable.
Lad's love, a bust of broom, hot a while and soon done.
Nobody wants to kiss when they are hungry.
Love and ambition admit no fellowship.
He loves you well who makes you weep.
Love built on beauty dies soon as beauty dies.
Love ceases to be a pleasure when it ceases to be a secret.
Love asks faith; faith firmness.
The sweets of love are mixed with tears.
Love is a sweet tyranny, because the lover endureth his torments, willingly.
Lovers remember all things.
A perfect love cannot be without equality.
Love, smoke, and a cough cannot be hid.
Love lives in cottages as well as in courts.
A lovers' quarrel is short-lived.
Love is blind, but sees afar.
One's sweetheart is never ugly.
Who has no children does not know what love is.
To be loved, be lovable (Ovid).

LOYALTY:
Loyalty is the holiest good in the human heart.

LUCK:
    If luck comes to you offer him a chair.
    Bad luck often brings good luck.
    Some run half-way to meet ill luck.

LUXURY:
    Luxury is like a wild beast, first made fiercer with tying and then let loose.
    Too much plenty makes the mouth dainty.
    Those who never had a cushion don't miss it.

M

MACHINERY:
    Machinery has greatly increased the number of well-to-do idlers.

MADNESS:
    A man of gladness seldom falls into madness.
    A mad beast must have a sober driver.
    The mad dog bites his master.
    Every mad man thinks all other men mad.
    With the mad it is necessary to be mad.
    We are all mad at some time or another.

MAID:
    Maidens must be mild and meek, swift to hear and slow to speak.
    All are good maids, but whence come the bad wives.
    A maid that laughs is half taken.
    A maid that talketh yieldeth.
    Maids should be seen and not heard.
    Maidens want nothing but husbands, and when they have them they want every thing.
    A maid and a virgin are not all one.
    Glass and a maid are ever in danger.
    The virtuous maid and the broken leg must stay at home.
    If a maid marries an old man, she becomes a young widow.

MAJORITY:
    One, on God's side, is a majority.

MAKE:
    You can't make an omelet without breaking some eggs.

MAKING THE BEST OF THINGS:
    A bite in the morning is better than nothing all day.
    A wooden leg is better than no leg.
    Better half an egg than an empty shell.

MALICE:
>Malice never spoke well.
>Malice drinketh its own poison.
>Malice is mindful.

MAMMON:
>Ye cannot serve God and Mammon (*Matt.*).

MAN:
>God divided man into many so that they may help each other.
>If you want to know a man travel with him.
>Every man has his weak side.
>Man that is born of woman is of few days and full of trouble (*Job*).
>Every man is his own enemy.
>Man being in honour abideth not; he is like the beast that perish (*Ps.*).
>A man like a watch, is to be valued for his going.
>Man is a wolf to man (*Latin*).
>Every man is best known to himself.
>An old man in a house is a good sign.
>Every man is either a fool or a physician to himself.
>A man is not known till he comes to honor.
>Every man is the son of his own works.
>A man is a lion in his own cause.
>Every man must carry his own cross.
>A man of words and not of deeds, is like a garden full of weeds.
>I am as bad as the worst, but Thank God I am as good as the best (*Whitman*).
>Man is a little soul carrying around a corpse (*Greek*).
>Man is a beast, when shame stands off from him (*Swinburne*).
>Man is but his mind.
>Man is heaven's masterpiece.
>An old man is a bed full of bones.
>Man is the only animal that blushes or needs to (*Mark Twain*).
>Man is a rope connecting animal and superman (*Nietzsche*).
>Man is the only animal that spits.
>Man is a reed, the weakest in nature, but he is a thinking reed (*Pascal*).
>Men have marble, women waxen minds (*Shakespeare*).
>Modes and customs vary, but human nature is the same (*Chesterfield*).
>I believe that man will not merely endure, he will prevail (*William Faulkner*).

No greater shame to man than inhumanity (*Spencer*).
The greatest enemy to man is man.
The only laughing animal is man.
Yes, all men are dust, but some are gold dust.
You are not wood, you are not stones, but men (*Shakespeare*).
It is more necessary to study men than books.
Man proposes and God disposes.
The noble man is only God's image.
Man is but breath and shadow (*Epictetus*).
Man is a reasoning animal.
A man is the child of his works.
A man is one who is faithful to his words.
Man's inhumanity to man makes countless thousands mourn.

MANNERS:
Manners make the man.
Other times, other manners.
Manners before meals (*O. Wilde*).
The society of good women is the foundation of good manners (*Goethe*).
Don't shake hands too eagerly (*Greek*).
Evil communications corrupt good manners.

MARKET:
Three women make a market, four a fair.
Three women and a goose make a market.

MARRIAGE:
It is not good that man should be alone (*Gen.*).
A married man turns his staff into a stake.
Marriage is honourable in all (*Heb.*).
Which, therefore God hath joined together, let no man put asunder (*Matt.*).
He that is needy when he is married shall be rich when he is buried.
To marry once is a duty, twice a folly, thrice a madness.
It is better to marry than to burn (*I Cor.*).
A man without a wife is but half a man.
Be sure before you marry of a house wherein to tarry.
A young man married is a young man marr'd (*Shakespeare*).
A good marriage should be between a blind wife and a deaf husband.
Better be half hanged than ill wed.
Hasty marriage seldom proveth well.

He that marries for wealth sells his liberty.
He that marries late marries ill.
It will not always be honeymoon.
Keep your eyes wide open before marriage and half shut afterwards (*Franklin*).
Marriage has many pains, but celibacy has no pleasure (*Johnson*).
Marriages are made in heaven.
Marriage is lottery.
Marry a wife of thine own degree.
Marry your son when you will, daughter when you can.
Wedding is destiny.
Where there is marriage without love, there will be love without marriage.
A poor man who marries a wealthy woman, gets a ruler and not a wife.
Don't praise marriage on the third day, but after the third year.
He that would an old wife wed, must eat an apple before he goes to bed.

MARTYR:
It is the cause, not the death, that makes the martyr.
The blood of the martyrs is the seed of the church (*Tertullian*).

MARVEL:
Marvel is the daughter of ignorance.

MASTER:
No man can serve two masters.
He that is a master must serve.
Like master like man.
Masters should be sometimes blind, and sometimes deaf.
Masters two will not do.
The master's eye is worth both his hands.
A sleepy master makes his servant a lout.
He that is master of himself will soon be the master of others.

MATCHMAKER:
Matchmakers often burn their fingers.

MAY-BE:
Every may-be hath a may-be-not.

MAXIM:
The maxims of men disclose their hearts.
A good maxim is never out of season.

MEANS:
Use the means and God will give the blessing.

MEASURE:
  Just scales and full measure injure no man.
  Measure for measure.
  Good weight and measure is heaven's treasure.
MEAT:
  Much meat, much maladies.
  A man has often more trouble to digest meat than to get it.
  One man's meat is another man's poison.
  It is good to be merry at meat.
  To a fully belly all meat is bad.
  Meat and cloth make the man.
  Broth made of cheap meat is tasteless.
  The nearer the bone, the sweeter the meat.
  Don't scald your tongue in other folks' broth.
MEDDLING:
  Never thrust your sickle into another's corn.
  It is not good to scald one's lips in other men's pottage.
  Put not your hand between the bark and the tree.
  Every fool will be meddling (*Prov.*).
MEDICINE:
  A disease known is half cured.
  Medicines are not meant to live on.
  An ounce of prevention is worth a pound of cure.
  Many dishes, many diseases.
  Many medicines, few cures.
  Meet the disease on its way.
  Many dishes, many diseases, many medicines.
  There are some medicines worse than the disease.
  What cures John makes George sick.
  For each disease there is a medicine.
MEEKNESS:
  Blessed are the meek for they shall inherit the earth.
  Meekness is not weakness.
MEETING:
  Men meet, mountains never.
MELANCHOLY:
  If there be a hell upon earth, it is to be found in the melancholy man's heart (*Barton*).
  He is a fool that is not melancholy once a day.
MEMORY:
  Memory, the warder of the brain (*Shakespeare*).

Memory is the treasury and guardian of all things.
Sorrow remembered, sweetness present joy.
All complain of want of memory but none of want of judgment.
Many a man fails to be a thinker, for the sole reason that his memory is too good.
We have all forgotten more than we remember.
There is no greater sorrow than to recall in misery the time when we were happy (*Dante*).

MEND:
Either mend or end.
Never too late to mend.

MENDING.
Mendings are honorable, rags are abominable.

MERCHANT:
There is no merchant who always gains.

MERCY:
Blessed are the merciful, for they shall obtain mercy (*Matt.*).
Mercy is better than vengeance.
Mercy to the criminal may be cruelty to the people.

MERIT:
Merit is worthier than fame.

MERRY:
It is good to be merry and wise.
It is good to be merry at meat.
It is merry when men meet.
The merry heart maketh a cheerful countenance.
Is any merry? Let him sing Psalms (*James*).

MESSENGER:
If you want a thing done go if not send.

MIDWIVES:
Hasty people will never make good midwives.

MIGHT:
I proclaim the might is right.
Might is not always right.
Might overcomes right.

MILK:
Don't cry over spilled milk.

MIND:
A strong body makes a mind strong.
Fat bodies, lean minds.
Little things please little minds.

A vacant life is open to all suggestions.
A hollow mountain returns the sounds.
It is good to rub and polish our minds against those of others.
It is the mind that enables not the blood.
Bodies without minds are as statues in the market place.
Wise men change their mind, fools never.
Mind is ever the ruler of the universe (*Plato*).
A wise man will be a master of his mind; fool its slave.
Bad mind, bad heart.
Pain of mind is worse than pain of body.

MINUTE:
Take care of the minutes and the hours will take care of themselves.

MIRTH:
Mirth and mischief are two things.
Mirth and motion prolong life.
In the time of mirth take heed.

MISCHIEF:
He that mischief hatcheth, mischief catcheth.
Little mischief too much.
Mischief comes by pounds, and goes away by ounces.
Women in mischief are wiser than men.
He prepares evil for himself, who plots mischief for others.

MISER:
A miser's death is the heir's holiday.
The miser is always poor.
The miser's teeth are frozen together by greed.
The rich miser and the fat goat are good after they are dead.

MISERY:
The memory of happiness makes misery woeful.
It is a little comfort to the miserable to have companions.
Misery acquaints a man with strange bed fellows (*Shakespeare*).

MISFORTUNE:
Misfortune tells us what fortune is.
Misfortunes when asleep are not to be awakened.
Misfortune unites men when the same thing is harmful to both.
Misfortune is friendless.

MISTAKE:
He who makes no mistakes makes nothing.
Mistakes are often the best teachers.
Mistakes occur through haste, never doing a thing leisurely.
I can pardon everybody's mistakes, but my own.

Wise men learn by other's mistakes, fools by their own.
Mistakes are easy, mistakes are inevitable but there is no mistake so great as the mistake of not going on (*Blake*).

MOB:
A mob has many heads but no brain.
Who does not mix with the crowd knows nothing.

MODERATION:
Only moderation gives charm to life.
Give me neither poverty nor riches (*Prov.*).
Stretch your legs according to your cover.
Moderation is best.
The golden rule in life is moderation in all things.
The best things carried to excess are wrong.

MODESTY:
Modesty is the beauty of women.
Modest dogs miss much meat.
Men may blush to hear what they were not ashamed to act.
Modesty cannot be taught, it must be born.

MONEY:
Money is the root of all evil.
Blessed is the man who has both mind and money, for he employs the latter well.
A man without money is a bow without an arrow.
A fool and his money are soon parted.
A hare may draw a lion with a golden cord.
A golden dart kills where it pleases.
Money, like manure, does no good till it is spread.
Gold goes in at any gate, except heaven's.
Gold will not buy everything.
He that gets money before he gets wit will be but a short time master of it.
A silver key can open an iron lock.
Money is a good servant but a bad master.
Talk is but talk, it is money that buys land.
He that serves God for money will serve the devil for better wages.
Put not your trust in money, put your money in trust (*Holmes*).
Would you know what money is, go borrow some.
Money talks.
Money is money, my little sonny, and a rich man's joke is always funny.
Ready money is really medicine.

When we have gold, we are in fear, when we have none we are in danger.

A full purse makes a man speak.

Money cures melancholy.

Ready money is ready medicine.

If you have money take a seat, if not stand on your feet.

Money makes a man laugh.

Money makes a man foolish.

When gold speaks, you hold your tongue.

MONUMENT:

Do not judge the dead by his monument.

The monuments of noble men are their virtues.

MORNING:

The morning hour has gold in its mouth.

An hour in the morning is worth two in the evening.

MORTALITY:

All flesh is grass, and all the goodness thereof is as the flower of the field (*Is.*).

All men think all men mortal but themselves.

All things are born of earth, all things earth takes again.

Remember that thou art mortal.

MOTHER:

Her children arise and call her blessed (*Prov.*).

One mother can satisfy ten children, but ten children not one mother.

Men are what their mothers make them.

A mother needs a large apron to cover her children's faults.

The mother's heart is always with her children.

What is home without a mother.

The mother's breath is sweet.

Good mother, child good.

Simply having children does not make mothers.

MOTHER-IN-LAW:

She is the happiest wife that marries the son of a dead mother.

Mother-in-law and daughter-in-law are a tempest and a hailstorm.

The mother-in-law remembers not that she was a daughter-in-law.

MOUNTAIN:

If you don't scale the mountain you can't view the plain.

A mountain and a river are good neighbors.

MOURNING:

It is better to go to the house of mourning than to go to the house of feasting (*Eccles*).

MOUSE:
>Don't make yourself a mouse or the cat will eat you.
>The mouse that has one hole is quickly taken.
>A mouse in time may bite in two a cable.

MOUTH:
>Out of the abundance of the heart, the mouth speaketh (Eccl.).
>A lying mouth is a sinking pit.
>Open thy mouth that I may know thee.
>Let your ears hear what your mouth says.
>Mouth and heart are wide apart.
>The heart of the fool is in his mouth, but the mouth of the wise man is in his heart.
>A wise head makes a close mouth.

MUCH:
>He that has many irons in the fire, some of them will cool.
>Even too much praise is a burden.
>Never too much of a good thing.
>Too much of a thing nauseates.

MUD:
>Muddy spring will have muddy streams.
>He who is in the mud likes to pull one into it.

MURDER:
>Murder may pass unpunished for a time, but tardy justice will take over the crime (Dryden).
>One murder makes a villain, millions a hero.

MUSIC:
>Music is the eye of the ear.
>Music is the speech of the angels.
>Music is the medicine of a troubled mind.
>Music, the only universal tongue.
>Music will not cure the toothache.

MUST:
>Must is a hard nut, but it has a sweet kernel.

N

NAIL:
>Hit the nail on the head.

NAME:
>Take away my good name, take away my life.
>A good name is rather to be chosen than great gifts (Prov.).

The name of the Lord is a strong tower (*Prov.*).
An ill wound is cured, not an ill name.
Who has a bad name is half hanged.

NATION:
That nation is worthless which does not joyfully stake everything in defense of her honor (*Schiller*).

NATURE:
Nature teaches us to love our friends, religion our enemies.
Nature, time and patience are the three great physicians.
The wolf may lose his teeth, but never his nature.
The heavens declare the glory of God and the firmament showeth his handiwork (*Ps.*).
Nature is a volume of which God is the author.
By nature all men are alike, but by education widely different (*Chinese*).
Nature is the art of God.
Never does nature say one thing and wisdom another.
Live according to nature.
Nature does nothing in vain.
What is natural is never disgraceful.
No men sleep so soundly as they that lay their heads upon nature's lap.
Every thing unnatural is imperfect.

NEAR:
The nearest the dearest.

NECESSITY:
Necessity is the mother of invention.
Necessity knows no law.
Need makes greed.
Necessity knows no shame.
Necessity makes an honest man a knave.
Necessity makes even the timid brave.

NEED:
Need sharpens the brain.
There is no need to blow what does not burn you.
Need teaches things unlawful.

NEEDLE:
A needle is not sharp at both ends.
Needle and thread are half clothing.

NEIGHBORS:
Thou shalt love thy neighbor as thyself.

A near neighbor is better than a far away brother.
Love your neighbor, yet pull not down your hedge.
Every man's neighbor is his looking glass.
We can live without our friends, but not without our neighbors.
The bad neighbor gives a needle without thread.
He who has a good neighbor has a good morning.

NEW:
Everything new is fine.

NEWS:
Good news may be told at any time, but ill in the morning.
As cold water to a thirsty stone, so's good news from a far country.
He knocks boldly who brings good news.
No news is good news.
Bad news is always true.

NIGHT:
Most men are begotten in the night.
Night is the mother of thought.
By night comes council to the wise.
The night is long to one awake in pain.
The night is a cloak for sinners.
What is done by night appears by day.
He that runs in the night stumbles.

NO AND YES:
Between a woman's yes or no,
There is not room for a pin to go.

NOBILITY:
The more noble, the more humble.
A noble soul alone can attract noble souls (*Goethe*).
The nobly born must nobly meet their fate.
True nobility is exempt from fear (*Shakespeare*).
Virtue alone is true nobility.

NOSE:
He that has a great nose thinks everybody is speaking of it.
Keep your nose out of another's mess.

NOW:
Now or never.

NUDITY:
Naked I was born, naked I am, I neither win nor lose.

NURSE:
The nurse is valued till the child has done sucking.

The nurse's tongue is privileged to talk.
With seven nurses a child will be without eye.
NUT:
He that would eat the kernel must crack the nut.

O

OATH:
Eggs and oaths are easily broken.
An unlawful oath is better broken than kept.
Children are to be deceived with sweets and men with oaths.
A true word needs no oath.
OBEDIENCE:
An obedient wife commands her husband.
Let them obey that know not how to rule.
Learn to obey before you command.
Obedience is the courtesy due to kings (Tennyson).
No one can rule except one who can be ruled.
Obedience is the mother of success, the wife of safety.
Obedience is yielded more readily to one who commands gently.
OBLIGATION:
Excess of obligation may lose a friend.
OBSERVATION:
Observation not old age brings wisdom.
OBSTINANCY:
Better go back than go wrong.
Better bow than break.
The wisest are the first to give way.
Stubborn heart shall fare evil at the last.
OCCASION:
An occasion lost cannot be redeemed.
OCCUPATION:
The vices of leisure are dispersed by occupation.
OLD:
A man is as old as his arteries.
You can't teach an old dog new tricks.
A man is as old as he feels, a woman as old as she looks.
ONE:
One foot is better than two crutches.
One swallow does not make a summer.
OPEN:
An open door may tempt a saint.

OPINION:
- So many heads, so many opinions.
- The foolish and the dead alone never change their opinions.
- The clash of opinion brings sparks of light.

OPPORTUNITY:
- An occasion lost cannot be redeemed.
- The mill cannot grind with the water that is past.
- Good things come to some when they are asleep.
- Make hay when the sun shines.
- Opportunity is the cream of time.
- Strike while the iron is hot.
- He who seizes the right moment is the right man (Goethe).
- Let us snatch our opportunity from the day.

OPPRESSION:
- He that oppresses the poor reproaches his maker.

OPTIMISM:
- The optimistic says half full, the pessimistic half empty.
- The diligent is an optimist, the lazy is a pessimist.

ORATORY:
- He is a good orator who convinces himself.
- Man becomes an orator, he is born eloquent.
- An orator's virtue is to speak the truth.

ORDER:
- Have a place for everything, and everything in its place.
- Let all things be done decently and in order (I Cor.).
- Set thine home in order (Is.).

ORPHAN:
- A fatherless child is half orphan, a motherless child a whole orphan.

OX:
- An ox is taken by the horns, and a man by the tongue.
- An old ox makes a straight furrow.
- When the ox falls many sharpen their knives.

P

PACT:
- Straw should make no pact with fire.

PAIN:
- No pains, no gains.
- Nothing to be got without pains but poverty.
- An hour of pain is as long as a day of pleasure.

Past pain is a pleasure.
Great pain and little gain will make a man soon weary.
If pains be a pleasure to you profit will follow.
No matter which finger you bite, it will hurt.
Sweet is pleasure after pain (*Dryden*).
Nothing is got without pains, but dirt and long nails.

PAINTING:
Good painting is like good cooking; it can be tasted, but not explained.
A picture is a poem without words.

PARADISE:
He that will enter into Paradise, must come with the right key.

PARDON:
Pardon all men but not thyself.
Pardon is the most glorious revenge.
It is more noble to pardon than to punish.
Pardoning the bad is injuring the good.
Pardon makes offenders.

PARENT:
Honour thy father and thy mother.
My son, hear the instruction of the father and forsake not the law of the mother.
If parents want honest children they should be honest themselves.

PARTING:
The best of friends must part.
To part is to die a little.

PARTNERSHIP:
When two men ride a horse one must ride behind.

PASSION:
The end of passion is the beginning of repentance.
Great passions are incurable diseases; the very remedies, make them worse (*Goethe*).

PAST:
Nothing is certain except the past.

PATIENCE:
Be patient like Job.
Patience wears out stones.
Be patient toward all men.
Grain by grain, the hen fills her belly.
Beware of the fury of a patient man (*Dryden*).
Patience is a plaster for all sores.

How poor are they that have not patience.
Patience opens all doors.
Let patience grow in your garden (Shakespeare).
Patience is a virtue.
Patience devours the devil.
Patience is the best medicine there is for a sick man.
Patience is the key to heaven.
Patience is bitter, but its fruits sweet.

PATRIOTISM:
He dies a glorious death who dies for his country.
It is sweet and glorious to die for one's nature land.
He loves his country best who strives to make it best.
A good citizen owes his life to his country.

PAYING:
He that payeth beforehand shall have his work ill done.
A good payer is master of another man's purse.
Pay well when you are served well.
He that cannot pay, let him pray.

PEACE:
Blessed are the peace makers (Matt.).
Peace feeds, war wastes.
Peace breeds, war consumes.
Peace makes plenty.
When a man finds no peace within himself, it is useless to seek it elsewhere.
A disarmed peace is weak.
Better a lean peace than a fat victory.
Better an egg in peace, than an ox in war.
Where there is peace God is.
Fame will be won in ear as well as in war.
Peace is liberty in tranquility.
They make it a desert and call it peace.
Where there is peace there is blessing.

PEASANT:
The peasant is peasant though he sleep till midday.

PEN:
A pen is more dangerous than a lion's paw.
The pen is mightier than the sword.
A sword less hurt does than a pen.
The pen is the tongue of life.

PENNY:
- Penny and penny laid up will be many.
- Take care of the pennies and the pounds will take care of themselves.
- Who heeds not a penny, shall never have any.
- Penny goes after penny, till Peter hasn't any.

PEOPLE:
- They who have put out the people's eyes reproach them of their blindness.
- The voice of the people is the voice of God.

PERFECTION:
- Be ye therefore perfect even as your father which is in heaven is perfect (*Matt.*).

PERSEVERANCE:
- Little strikes fell great oaks.
- Persevere and never fear.
- Troy was not taken in a day.
- Rome was not built in a day.
- In time a mouse will gnaw through a cable.
- An oak is not felled with one blow.
- Perseverance performs greater works than strength.
- Step after step the ladder is ascended.

PESSIMIST:
- A pessimist thinks everybody as nasty as himself (*G. B. Shaw*).
- A pessimist says half the bottle is empty, the optimist says the bottle is half filled.

PHILANTHROPY:
- Be not weary in well doing (*II Thess.*).
- Blessed is he that considereth the poor (*Ps.*).
- I was eyes to the blind and feet was I to the lame (*Job*).
- He who bestows his goods upon the poor, shall have as much again as ten times more (*Bunyan*).
- Not what we give, but what we share, for the gift without the giver is bare (*Lowell*).
- The hands that help are holier than the lips that pray (*Ingersoll*).
- The most acceptable service of God is doing good to men (*Franklin*).
- We praise those who love their fellow-men (*Aristotle*).
- Only those live who do good (*Tolstoy*).
- Wipe the nose of your neighbor's son, and take into your house.

PHILOSOPHY:
    Many talk like philosophers and live like fools.
    Let the philosopher be wise for himself.
    The true medicine of mine is philosophy.
    To enjoy freedom be the slave of philosophy.

PHYSICIAN:
    The best physicians are Dr. Diet, Dr. Quiet, Dr. Merryman.
    Conceal not the truth from thy physician and lawyer.
    Honor a physician before you have need of him.
    Physician, heal thyself.
    God heals and the physician hath the thanks.
    Every man is a fool or a physician at forty.
    He is a fool that makes his physician his heir.
    More danger from the physician than from the disease.
    An old physician, a young lawyer.
    Happy is the physician who is called at the end of sickness.

PICTURES:
    Pictures are the books of the unlearned.

PIETY:
    Piety is the foundation of all virtue.

PILLOW:
    Our pillow should be our consellor.

PILOT:
    A pilot is not chosen for riches, but for his knowledge.

PINCH:
    Everyone knows where the shoe pinches.

PINE:
    The pine wishes herself a shrub when the axe is at her root.

PIT:
    Who diggeth a pit for his brother, he himself falls in it (*Prov.*).

PITCHER:
    Whether the pitcher strike the stone, or the stone the pitcher, woe to the pitcher.

PITY:
    He that hath pity on the poor lendeth to the poor (*Prov.*).
    Pity cures envy.
    Foolish pity spoils a city.

PLACE:
    The place is dignified by the doer's deed.
    There is no greater immorality than occupy a place you cannot fill (*Napoleon*).

It is not the place that grace men, but men the place.
Nothing is more annoying than a low man in a high place.

PLANNING:
Man proposes, God disposes.

PLEASE:
He that please all and himself too, undertakes what he cannot do.
Nobody can please everybody.
He that all men please shall never find ease.

PLEASURE:
Pleasure is a sin, and sometimes sin is a pleasure (*Byron*).
If you long for pleasure, you must labor hard to get.
God made all pleasures innocent.
No pleasure without pain.
Sweet is pleasure after pain (*Dryden*).
Never pleasure without repentance.
Stolen pleasures are sweet.
Pleasures are transient, honors are immortal.
A wise man resists pleasure, a fool is a slave to them.
Excess of delight palls the appetite.
Pleasure hours fly fast.

PLENTY:
He who of plenty will take no heed, shall find default in time of need.
Plenty brings pride, pride glee, glee pain, pain peace, and peace plenty.

PLOUGH:
He that by the plough would thrive, himself must either hold or drive.
It is folly to put the plough in front of the oxen.

POCKET:
The poor man throws away what the rich man puts in his pocket.

POET:
Poets utter great and wise things, which they do not themselves understand (*Plato*).
All poets are mad (*Burton*).
A poet is born, not made.

POISON:
One man's meat is another man's poison.

POLITENESS:
Politeness is to do and say, the kindest things in the kindest way.
One never loses anything by politeness.

POMP:
>All our pomp the earth covers.

POOR:
>The poor ye always have with thee (Matt.).
>Poor men seek meat for their stomachs, rich men stomach for their meat.
>A poor man has few acquaintances.
>Every poor man is counted a fool.
>God helps the poor, the rich can help themselves.
>God help the rich for the poor can beg.
>As poor as a church mouse.

POPULARITY:
>The popularity of a bad man is as treacherous as himself.

POSSESSION:
>A bird in the hand is worth two in the bush.

POVERTY:
>Blessed be ye poor, for yours is the Kingdom of God (Luke).
>Bare walls make giddy housewives.
>If thou be poor, thy brother hateth thee.
>Poverty is no vice, but an inconvenience.
>Poverty is no sin.
>If you are poor distinguish yourself by your virtues, if rich by your good deeds.
>A poor man is not believed though he speaks the truth.
>No man should know poverty, but he who is poor (St. Bernard).
>Nothing is more luckless than a poor man.
>Poverty makes strange bedfellows.
>There are two families in the world, the Haves and the Have Nots.
>Poverty is the mother of health.
>He is a wise man that can wear poverty decently.
>The poor man is despised everywhere.
>Patience with poverty is all a poor man's remedy.
>The devil dances in an empty pocket.
>Wrinkled purses make wrinkled faces.
>When poverty comes in at the door, love flies out of the window.

POWERS:
>The powers that be are ordained of God (Rom.).
>Increase of power begets increase of wealth.
>A partnership with powerful is never safe.
>Lust of power is the strangest of all passions.

Power weakeneth the wicked.
The highest power may be lost by misrule.

PRACTICE:
Practice makes perfect.
Practice well if you excel (*Chinese*).

PRAISE:
Praise day at night and life at the end.
Praise the sea but keep on land.
Every body claims his labor sweet.
Every man claims his yoghurt sweet.
Good things should be praised.
One has only to die to be praised.
He that praises publicly will slander privately.
Usually we praise only to be praised.
Let every man praise the bridge he goes on.
Praise to the face is open disgrace.
An honest man is hurt by praise unjustly bestowed.
He who loves praise loves temptation.

PRAYER:
All things whatsoever ask in prayer, believing, ye shall receive (*Matt.*).
Ask and it shall be given you; seek and ye shall find; knock and it shall be opened unto you (*Matt.*).
Who wants to pray he must fast and be clean, and fat his soul and make his body lean (*Chaucer*).
The prayer of faith shall save the sick (*James*).
Watch and pray (*Mark*).
Your Father knoweth what things ye have need of, before ye ask Him (*Matt.*).
The Satan trembles when he sees, the weakest saint upon his knees (*Cowper*).
Common people do no praying; they only beg (*G. B. Shaw*).
He who ceases to pray ceases to prosper.
A short prayer enters heaven.
More things are wrought by prayer than this world dreams of (*Ten*).
Prayer ardent opens Heaven (*Young*).
Danger is cause for prayers.
Prayer should be the key of the day and the lock of the night.
Who goes to bed, and doth not pray, maketh two nights to every day.

Who prays without trust cannot hope to have his prayer answered.
They never sought in vain that sought the Lord aright (Burns).
A grateful thought toward heaven is a complete prayer.
Fear drives to prayer.
Rather go run with good men than pray with bad.
Who rises from prayer a better man, his prayer is answered.
Prayers go up and blessings come down.
Prayer moves the hand that moves the world.
God is always at leisure to do good to those who seek it.
Prayer knocks till the door is opened.

PREACHING:
Practice what you preach.
None preaches better than the ant, and she says nothing (Franklin).
A good example is the best sermon.
Preach not because you have to say something but because you have something to say.
Preachers say, Do as I say, not as I do.
He preaches well that lives well.

PRECOCITY:
Soon learnt, soon forgotten, soon ripe, soon rotten.

PREPAREDNESS:
One sword keeps another in sheath.
Who carries a sword, carries peace.
If you want peace be prepared for war.

PRESENT:
Better an egg today than a hen tomorrow.
No time like the present.

PRESS:
Three hostile newspapers are more to be feared than a thousand bayonets (Napoleon).
When the press is free and every man able to read, all is safe (Jefferson).

PREVENTION:
An ounce of prevention is better than a pound of cure (Raleigh).

PRIDE:
Pride goeth before destruction, and a haughty spirit before a fall (Prov.).
When pride comes then cometh shame (Prov.).
The pride of the poor does not endure.
As proud as a peacock.

Pride and grace, dwell never in one place.
A man may be poor in purse, yet proud in spirit.
Pride and gout are seldom cured throughout.
Pride breakfasted with plenty, dineth with poverty, and supped with infamy.
Pride goes before, shame follows after.
God is the enemy of the proud.
Pride and conceit were the original sin of men.

PRIEST:
The priest is always with the herd and against the individual.

PRINCE:
A prince's greatest virtue is to know his own.

PRIORITY:
It is better to be the head of a lizard than the tail of a lion.

PRISON:
No man loveth his fetters, be they made of gold.

PROBABILITIES:
A thousand probabilities do not make one truth.

PROCRASTINATION:
Never put off till tomorrow what can be done today.

PRODIGAL:
The prodigal robs his heir, the miser himself.

PROFIT:
Profit is better than fame.

PROGRESS:
He who moves not forward goes backward.

PROHIBITION:
Things forbidden have a secret charm.
Forbidden wine sells twice as dear.

PROMISE:
Vows made in storms are forgotten in calms.
An acre of performance is worth a whole land of promise.
A man apt to promise is apt to forget.
Don't put it in my ear, but in my head.
He who gives fair words feeds you with an empty spoon.
They promise mountains, and perform molehills.
Take heed, girl, of the promise of a man, for it will run like a crab.
A promise neglected is an untruth told.
A long tongue is a sign of a short hand.

PROOF:
    Prove all things, hold fast that which is good (I Thess.).
    The proof of the pudding is in the eating.
    What is now proved, was once only imagined.
    One must not hang a man by his looks.
PROPERTY:
    If a man own land, the land owns him.
PROPORTION:
    Burn not your house to fight away the mouse.
    Send not for a hatchet to break open an egg with.
    Take not a musket and kill a butterfly.
PROSPERITY:
    A full cup is hard to carry.
    Prosperity forgets father and mother.
    He who swells in prosperity will shrink in adversity.
    Adversity reveals genius, prosperity hides it.
    In time of prosperity friends will be plenty; in time of adversity not one among twenty.
    In the days of prosperity be joyful, but in the day of adversity consider (Eccl.).
    Prosperity is a great teacher, adversity a greater.
    Prosperity discovers vice; adversity, virtue.
    Prosperity makes friends, adversity tries them.
    In prosperity caution, in adversity patience.
    Profits little and often fulls the purse.
    Plenty is the child of peace.
    Prosperous men seldom mend their faults.
    We are corrupted by prosperity.
PROVERBS:
    Patch grief with proverbs (Shakespeare).
    Proverbs are the wisdom of the streets.
    The genius, wit, and spirit of a nation are discovered in its proverbs (Bacon).
    A short saying often contains much wisdom.
    A proverb is a short sentence based on long experience.
    There is no proverb which is not true.
    A proverb is the wit of one and the wisdom of many.
    A good maxim is never out of season.
PROVIDENCE:
    God provides for him that trusteth.
    If you leap into a well, providence is not bound to fetch you out.

God builds the nest of a blind bird (Turkish).
He who gives us teeth will give us bread.
Providence cares for every hungry mouth.

PROVISION:
Lay up for a rainy day.
The first years of a man's life must make provision for the last.

PRUDENCE:
The prudent man looketh well to his going (Prov.).
Use another's foot to kick a dog.
A stitch in time saves nine.
The prudent seldom err (Chinese).
Beware of a mule's hind foot, a dog's tooth, and a woman's tongue.
You can't hold two melons in one hand.
The brave man is the prudent one.
Precaution is better than cure.
Better to go on foot than ride and fall.
Put your trust in God, and keep your powder dry (Cromwell).
Whose house is of glass must not throw stones at another.
Praise the mountains but love the plains.
A prudent men does not make the goat his gardener.
We accomplish more by prudence than by force.
Grasp not at much for fear thou losest all.
Look before you leap (Spanish).
Call the Bear "uncle" till you are safe.

PUNCTUALITY:
Punctuality is the soul of the business.

PUNISHMENT:
A whip for the horse, a bridle for the ass, and a rod for the fool's back (Prov.).
Let those who have deserved their punishment bear it patiently.
He that spareth his rod hateth his son (Prov.).
Let the punishment be equal with the offence.
Who punishes one threatens a hundred.
Let the ruler be slow to punish, swift to reward.

PURITY:
Blessed are the pure in heart for they shall see God (Matt.).
Unto the pure all things are pure (Titus).

PURPOSE:
A good archer is known not by its armour but by his aim.

PURSE:
>A full purse never lacks friends.
>According to your purse, let your mouth speak.
>That is but an empty purse that is full of other man's money.

Q

QUACK:
>Trust not yourself to a quack when you are sick.

QUALITY:
>Great qualities make great men.
>There was never a good knife made of bad steel.

QUARREL:
>A good sword's man is not a quarreller.
>A quarrelsome man has no good neighbors.
>Quarrelsome dogs get dirty.
>
>Those who in quarrels interpose,
>Must often wipe a bloodly nose.
>
>Paintings and fightings are best seen at a distance.
>Avoid quarrels causeth by wine.
>Quarrels never could belong, if on one side only lay the wrong.

QUESTION:
>He that nothing questioneth, nothing learneth.
>Never answer a question until asked.
>Questions are never indiscreet, answers sometimes are (O. Wilde).
>Hard questions must have hard answers.
>It is not that every question deserves answer.
>A fool man asks more questions in an hour than a wise man will answer in seven years.

QUICK:
>Quick and good go not well together.

QUIET:
>Better is a dry morsel and quietness therewith, than a house full of sacrifice with strife (Prov.).
>Some times quiet is an unquiet thing.

QUOTATIONS:
>The wisdom of the wise and the experience of the ages.
>A fine quotation is a diamond on the finger of a man of wit and a pebble in the hand of a fool.

R

RACE:
> The race is got by running.

RAGS:
> Better go to heaven in rags than to hell in embroidery.

RAIN:
> He sends rain on the just and on the unjust (*Matt.*).
> Much rain wears the marble.
> One already wet does not feel the rain.

RAINBOW:
> The rainbow shall be a covenant between me and the earth (*Gen.*).

RAT:
> An old rat easily finds a hole.

READING:
> I love to lose myself in other men's minds.
> Life is too short to read inferior books.
> Read, mark, learn and inwardly digest (*Book of Common Prayer*).
> Reading furnishes the mind only with materials of knowledge (*Locke*).
> Reading maketh a full man (*Bacon*).
> It is not wide reading but useful reading that tends to excellence.
> Letters enter with the blood.
> He that loves reading has everything within his reach.

READY:
> He who is not ready today, will be less so tomorrow.

REASON:
> A man without reason is a beast in season.
> Reason hinders the man.
> Reason rules all things.

REBUKE:
> Open rebuke is better than secret hatred.

RECEIVE:
> The receiver is as bad as the thief.

REFORM:
> Every generation needs regeneration.
> Reform must come from within, not from without (*Gibbons*).
> Him who reforms, God assists.

REFUSE:
> Some refuse roast meat, and later long for the smoke of it.

REGRET:
   The mind longs for what it has missed (*Latin*).
RELATIVES:
   Dine with thy aunt, but not everyday.
RELIGION:
   All religion relates to life, and the life of religion is to do good (*Swedenborg*).
   A man without a religion is like a beast without bridle.
   Many have quarrelled about religion that never practiced it.
   Religion lies more in work than in talk.
   Religion is the elder sister of philosophy (*Lendor*).
   Those who worship God merely for fear, would worship the devil should he appear.
   Religion without joy is no religion.
REMEDY:
   There is a remedy for all things but death.
   If there be a remedy why worry? If there be no remedy, why worry?
REPENTANCE:
   Joy shall be in heaven over one sinner that repenteth (*Luke*).
   Repentance is good but innocence is better.
   A death bed repentance seldom reaches to restitution.
   It is never too late to repent.
   Repentance is the virtue of weak minds.
   There is no repentance in the grave.
REPROOF:
   Open rebuke is better than secret love (*Prov.*).
   Reprove not a scorner, lest he hate thee, rebuke a wise man, and he will love thee (*Prov.*).
   Reprove never does a wise man harm.
   Who reproves the lame must go upright.
REPUTATION:
   A good fame is better than a good face.
   Get a good name and go to sleep.
   A wounded reputation is seldom cured.
   A good reputation is a fair estate.
   A good name endureth for ever (*Apoc.*).
   Reputation is the life of the mind as breath is the life of the body.
   A good name is rather to be chosen than great riches (*Prov.*).
   Get a good name and you may lie a-bed.

Good name in man and woman is the immediate jewel of their soul (*Shakespeare*).

He that hath an ill name is half-hanged.

Take away my good name, and take away my life.

RESIGNATION:

It is no use crying over spilt milk.

RESOLUTION:

Never tell your resolution beforehand.

The more things a man is ashamed of, the more respectable he is (*G. B. Shaw*).

RESPECT:

Respect man and he will do the same.

RESPONSIBILITY:

Few are fit to be intrusted with themselves.

One of the greatest misfortunes of respectable people is that they are cowards (*Voltaire*).

Responsibility should be shouldered, you cannot carry it under your arm.

REST:

Too much rest itself becomes a pain.

Rest is won only by work.

If I rest, I rust.

RETRIBUTION:

Whatsoever a man soweth, that shall he also reap (*Gal.*).

As you salute you will be saluted.

God stays long, but strikes at last.

REVENGE:

Revenge is mine; I will repay, said the Lord (*Rom.*).

Revenge is a diet that should be eaten cold.

Living well is the best revenge.

Revenge is a morsel for God.

Revenge in cold blood is the devil's own act and deed.

A man that studieth revenge keeps his own wounds green (*Bacon*).

The noblest vengeance is to forgive.

To forget a wrong is the best revenge.

REVOLUTION:

An hour may destroy what an age was building.

RICH:

Much coin, much care.

He that maketh haste to be rich shall not be innocent (*Prov.*).

A man that keeps riches and enjoys them not is like an ass that carries gold and eats thistles.
The rich follow wealth, the poor the rich.
For one rich man content, there are a hundred not.
The rich knows not who is his friend.
It is better to live rich, than to die rich.
The rich need not beg a welcome.
Rich men's spots are covered with money.
Riches serve a wise man but command a fool.
As money grows, greed for greater riches follows after.
Better God than gold.
Lay not up for yourselves treasures upon earth, where moth and rust doth corrupt (*Matt.*).
He is rich enough that needeth neither to flatter nor to borrow.
The rich man's wealth is most enemy unto his health.
Morals are corrupted by the worship of riches.
We all ask whether he is wealthy; none whether he is good.

RIDING:
Better ride an ass that carries me than a horse that throws me.

RIGHT:
Be sure you are right, then go ahead (*Crockett*).
Right is with the strongest.
No one is always right.
I see the right and approve it, yet I follow the wrong (*Ovid*).
Right wrongs no man.
Where force prevails, right perishes.
Better to do right without thanks, than wrong without punishment.
The righteous shall flourish as the palm tree.

RISING:
The early bird catches the fly.
Go to bed with the lamb, and rise with the lark.
Who rises late must trod all day.
The early bird gets the late one's breakfast.
Early to bed and early to rise, makes a man healthy, wealthy and wise.

RIVER:
Where the river is deepest it makes least noise.
Follow the river and you will get to the sea.

ROAD:
I will find a road or make one (*Hannibal*).
Keep the common road and thou art safe.

ROB:
    To rob a robber is not robbery.
ROLLING:
    A rolling stone gathers no moss.
ROME:
    All roads lead to Rome.
    Rome was not built in one day.
    When you are in Rome do as Romans do.
ROPE:
    Name not a rope in the house of him that was hanged.
ROSE:
    The fairest and the sweetest rose, in time must fade and beauty lose.
    No rose without a thorn.
    Roses and maidens soon lose their bloom.
    An onion will not produce a rose.
    He that plants thorns must never expect to gather roses.
    When the rose dies the thorn is left behind.
RUDENESS:
    To a rude ass, a rude keeper.
RULER:
    Unjust rule, never endure.
    The desire to rule is stronger than all other passions.
    Let the ruler be slow to punish, swift to reward.
RUMORS:
    In calamity any rumor is believed.
    Rumor is a great traveller.
RUST:
    Better to wear out than to rust out.

S

SACK:
    Old sacks want much patching.
    Nothing can come out of a sack but what is in it.
SADNESS:
    Sadness and gladness succeed each other.
SAFETY:
    There is always safety in valour.
SAINT:
    All are not saints that go to church.
    Blessed in the sight of the Lord is the death of saints (Ps.).

SALT:
Of all smells, bread; of all tastes, salt.
A man must eat a peck of salt with his friends before he knows them.
SALVATION:
The knowledge of sin is the beginning of salvation.
I know that my redeemer liveth (*Job*).
Salvation is from God only.
SAVING:
Penny and penny laid up will be many.
Saving comes too late when you get to the bottom.
From saving comes having.
Prepare in youth for your old age.
Husbands can earn, but only wives can save.
SAYING:
Say no ill of the year till it is past.
Easier said than done.
What is said cannot be unsaid.
SCALD:
Scald not your lips in another man's pottage.
SCANDAL:
A lie has no legs, but a scandal has wings.
Gossips are frogs—they drink and talk.
SCAR:
A scar nobly got is a good livery of honour (*Shakespeare*).
SCHOLAR:
The ink of the scholar is more sacred than the blood of the martyr (*Arab*).
SCHOOL:
Every good scholar is not a good school master.
SCIENCE:
Science is organized knowledge.
Wonder is the seed of knowledge.
Much science, much sorrow.
Science is the topography of ignorance (*Holmes*).
Science is the cemetery of dead ideas.
SCOLDS:
Husbands are in heaven where wives scold not.
SCRATCH:
I scratch where it itches.
SEA:
All the rivers run into the sea, yet the sea is not full.

The sea refuses no river.
In a calm sea every man is a pilot.
Let him who knows not how to pray go to the sea or ride in an aeroplane.

SECRET:
The secret is thy prisoner; if thou let it go, thou art a prisoner to it.
He who tells a secret is another's servant.
The secret is a weapon and a friend.
If you want to keep your secret from an enemy, tell it not to a friend.
Secrecy is the seal of speech.
Three men may keep a secret, if two of them are dead.
Two things a man cannot hide; that he is drunk and that he is in love.
He who keeps his own secret avoids much mischief.

SEEK:
Seek and you shall find, knock and it shall be opened to you.

SELF:
He is a slave of the greatest slave who serves nothing but himself.

SELF-CONCEIT:
There is more hope of a fool, than of him that is wise in his own conceit (*Prov.*).

SELF CONFIDENCE:
Let every man's hope be in himself.

SELF-CONSCIOUS:
He that has a great nose thinks everybody is speaking of it.

SELF CONTROL:
Few are fit to be intrusted with themselves.
He that is master of himself will soon be master of others.
Rule lust, temper, tongue, and bridle the belly.
He is strong who conquers others, he who conquers himself is mighty.

SELF DENIAL:
Deny self for self's sake.

SELF DEPRECIATION:
Who makes himself a sheep will be eaten by the wolves.

SELF HELP:
God reaches us good things by our own hands.
If you want a thing well done do it yourself.
God helps them who help themselves.

When everyone takes care of himself, care is taken of all.
Help yourself and your friends will help you.
SELF KNOWLEDGE:
We know what we are, but not what we may be (Shakespeare).
I know myself better than any doctor can (Ovid).
What you think of yourself is much more important than what others think of you.
Every man is best known to himself.
The best mirror is an old friend.
He who wears the shoe best knows where it pinches.
SELF LOVE:
Generally we love ourselves more than we hate others.
SELF PRAISE:
Self praise is no recommendation.
Every cook praiseth his own broth.
He that praiseth himself, spattereth himself.
Self praise is not honor.
Neither praise nor disprove thyself, thine actions serve the turn.
SELF PRESERVATION:
He kills a man that saves not his life when he can.
SELF RESPECT:
Respect yourself most of all.
Self respect is the corner stone of virtue.
Respect yourself; others will respect you.
SELF SACRIFICE:
Present your bodies as living sacrifices, holy, acceptable unto God (Rom.).
SELF TORTURE:
He that is ill to himself will be good to nobody.
SELFISHNESS:
He is unworthy to love who lives only for himself.
Every man for himself and God for us all.
He set my house on fire only to roast his eggs.
SELL:
Sell me dear and measure me fair.
SENSE:
Common sense is not so common.
SENSUALITY:
Serving one's own passions is the greatest slavery.
SERMON:
Funeral sermons—lying sermons.

SERVANT:
- He that is greatest among you shall be your servant.
- A servant is known by his master's absence.
- A servant that is diligent and good, must sing at his work like a bird in the wood.
- Bad servants wound their master's fame.
- Great men's servants think themselves great.
- When the maid leaves the door open, the cat's in fault.
- If you pay not a servant his wages, he will pay himself.
- If you would have good servants, see that you be good masters.
- Few men have been admired of their servants.
- A good saver is a good server.
- Who wishes to be ill served, let him keep many servants.
- Do not be ready to believe, a wife complaining of servants.
- A tongue of a bad servant is his worst part.

SERVICE:
- They serve God well who serve his creatures.

SERVITUDE:
- Many kiss the hand they wish to cut off.

SHADOW:
- Our days on earth are as a shadow.

SHAME:
- He that has no shame has no conscience.
- Who has no shame before men, has no fear of God.
- Man is a beast when shame stands off from him.
- Where shame is there is fear (*Milton*).
- Shame lost, honour lost.
- Shame arises more from fear of men than of God.

SHARP:
- Beware how you give away an edged tool, unto a young child and unto a fool.

SHEEP:
- The dust raiseth by the sheep does not choke the wolf.
- The sheep has no choice when in the jaws of the wolf (*Chinese*).
- The death of the wolf is the health of the sheep.
- He who has sheep has fleece.

SHIP:
- Two captains sink the ship.
- Ships fear fire more than water.
- A great ship asks deep waters.

SHOE:
　　Better cut the shoe than pinch the feet.
SHOP:
　　Keep thy shop and thy shop will keep thee.
SHREW:
　　Little peace where the hen crows and the cock is mute.
SICKNESS:
　　Sickness comes by tons and leaves by ounces.
　　Sickness is every man's master.
　　Sickness comes on horse-back, but goes away on foot.
　　Sickness shows us what we are.
　　The room of sickness is the room of devotion.
SILENCE:
　　Silence is a fine jewel for a woman, but it is a little worn.
　　Better to remain silent and be thought a fool, than to speak out and remove all doubt.
　　Speech is often repented, silence never.
　　Silence seldom hurts.
　　He is not a fool who knows when to hold his tongue.
　　There is a time for speaking and a time for being still.
　　He that speaks sows, and he that holds his peace gathers.
　　Hear, see, and be silent if you wish to live in peace.
　　Silence is wisdom when speaking is folly.
　　Silence is the sanctuary of truth.
　　When you have nothing to say, say nothing.
　　Do you wish people to think well of you? Don't speak.
　　Wise men say nothing in dangerous times.
　　It is sad when men have neither wit to speak, nor judgment to hold their tongues.
　　Silent people are dangerous.
　　No wisdom like silence.
　　Silence is the wit of fools.
　　Keep shut the door of thy mouth even from the wife of thy bosom.
　　Silence is safest for one who distrusts himself.
　　No one betrays himself by silence.
　　All things except silence bring repentance.
　　Beware of a silent dog and still water.
　　Be silent or let thy words be worth more than silence.
　　Silence is also speech.
　　Deep vengeance is the daughter of deep silence.

Dumb dogs are dangerous.
Good rights the man that keeps silent (Persian).
SILVER:
A silver key can open an iron lock.
SIMPLICITY:
Blessed are the simple, for they shall have peace.
Nothing is more simple than greatness (Emerson).
SIN:
God hardens the hearts of sinners.
Without knowledge there is no sin.
Sin writes histories; goodness is silent (Goethe).
Who is not ashamed of his sins, sins double.
All that defiles comes from within.
The righteous sometimes pays for the sinner.
To sin is human; but to persevere in sin is satanic.
God be merciful to me, a sinner (Luke).
Fear nothing but sin.
Be sure your sin will find you out (Numbers).
Fools make a mock of sin (Prov.).
The wages of sin is death (Romans).
He that is without sin among you, let him cast the first stone (John).
Every man carries the bundle of his sins upon his own back.
Little sins make room for great.
One leak will sink a ship, and one sin will destroy a sinner (Bunyan).
Few love to hear the sins they love to act.
A sin confessed, is half forgiven.
Some rise by sin, and some by virtue fall (Shakespeare).
Sins are not known till they be acted.
Old sin makes new shame.
The longer thread of life we spin, the more occasion still to sin (Herrick).
SINCERITY:
Sincerity is the parent of truth.
The sincere alone can recognize sincerity.
Sincerity gives wings to power.
The foundation of that steadfastness and constancy which we seek in friendship is sincerity, for nothing is steadfast which is not sincere (Cicero).

SING:
　He who sings frightens away his ills.

SKILL:
　All things require skill but an appetite.
　Skill is stronger than strength.

SLANDER:
　Slander, whose sting is sharper than a sword's (Shakespeare).
　A generous heart repairs a slanderous tongue (Homer).
　If slander be a snake, it is a winged one; it flies as well as creeps.
　Speak no ill of a friend, nor even of an enemy.
　Thy friend has a friend, and thy friend's friend has a friend, so be discreet.
　If you slander a dead man, you stab him in his grave.
　Slander slays three persons; the speaker, the spoken, and the spoken of.

SLAVERY:
　If slavery is not wrong, nothing is wrong (Lincoln).
　The blow that liberates the slave, sets the master free (Roche).
　Slavery is as ancient as war, and war as human nature (Voltaire).
　Retain a free mind, though a slave, and slave thou shalt not be (Greek).

SLEEP:
　One hour's sleep before midnight is worth three afterwards.
　The sleep of a laboring man is sweet (Eccl.).
　Sleep is better than medicine.
　After lunch a short nap, after supper a short walking (Arabic).
　I never sleep comfortably except when I am at sermon (Rabelais).
　No one when asleep is good for anything.
　He sleeps enough who does nothing.
　Blessings on him that first invented sleep (Cervantes).
　Sleep is the best cure for waking trouble.
　Sleep to the sick is half health.
　In sleep what difference is there between Solomon and a fool?

SLIP:
　Better slip with foot than tongue.

SLOW:
　Be slow to promise, quick to perform.
　Slow and steady wins the race.
　Slow but sure.

SLUGGARD:
>Go to the ant, thou sluggard,
>Consider her ways and be wise (*Prov.*).

SMALL:
>Small axes fell great trees.
>A small cloud may hide both sun and moon.
>A small hurt in the eye is a great one.
>Small things make base men proud (*Shakespeare*).

SMILE:
>A tender smile is sorrow's only balm.
>A smile is a light in the window of a face which shows that the heart is at home.
>A man without a smiling face must not study medicine, nor open a shop.
>There's a dagger in men's smiles (*Shakespeare*).

SMOKE:
>No smoke without some fire.

SNAKE:
>Serpents lie where flowers grow.
>Draw the snake out of the hole with another's hand.
>Put a frozen snake in your bosom and it will sting when it is warm.

SNEER:
>Sneer not at that which you cannot rival.

SNOW:
>Whether you boil snow or pound it, you can have but water of it.

SOCIETY:
>Man is a social animal.
>The wise man flees society for fear of being bored.

SOLDIERS:
>The greatest general is he who makes the fewest mistakes (*Napoleon*).
>The worse the man the better the soldier (*Napoleon*).
>An army like a serpent goes on its belly (*Napoleon*).
>A good soldier talks of success, not of failure.
>It is the blood of the soldier which makes the general great.
>What makes the real general is to have clean hands.
>I never expect a soldier to think (*G. B. Shaw*).
>Soldiers in peace are like chimneys in summer.

SOLITUDE:
>A solitary man is either a brute or an angel.

Woe to him that is alone when he falleth (*Eccl.*).
Solitude is the best nurse of wisdom.
Woe unto them that cannot bear to be alone.
A solitude is the audience chamber of God.
One would not be alone, even in Paradise.

SON:
A wise son maketh a glad father, but a foolish son is the heavens of his mother (*Prov.*).
The son disgraces himself when he blames his father.
Good wombs have borne bad sons (*Shakespeare*).
He that brings his son to nothing breeds a thief.
Like father, like son.
Every man is the son of his own works.
A son who marries gives his wife a contract and his mother a divorce.

SON-IN-LAW:
He who has gold can choose his son-in-law.
I can see by my daughter's face when the devil takes hold of my son-in-law.

SOON:
Soon got, soon spent.

SORROW:
A day of sorrow is longer than a month of joy.
Sorrow hath killed many, and there is no profit therein (*Apoc.*).
Earth has no sorrow that Heaven cannot heal.
The busy bee has no time for sorrow.
When sorrow is asleep wake it not.
Two in distress, makes sorrow less.
Rejoice not in another's sorrow (*Turkish*).

SOUL:
For what a man profits, if he shall gain the whole world and lose his own soul (*Matt.*).
The body is sooner dressed than the soul.
Be careless in your dress if you must, but keep a tidy soul (*Mark Twain*).
Little bodies have great souls.
The soul is not where it lives, but where it loves.
The soul alone renders us noble.
There is a divinity within our breast.
The soul needs few things, the body many.
It is more necessary to cure the soul than the body.

Lack of wealth is easily repaired, but poverty of soul is irreparable.
The soul is immortal and is clothed in many bodies (*Plato*).

SOW:
He that sows thistles shall reap prickles.
He who sows some money will reap poverty.
They have sown the wind, and they shall reap the whirlwind.

SPARE:
Too late to spare, when the pocket is bare.
He that spareth his rod hateth his son (*Prov.*).

SPARK:
A spark will set a whole city on fire.

SPARROW:
Sparrows fight for corn which is none of their own.

SPEECH:
Speak fitly, or be wise silently.
Hear first, speak afterwards.
Speak well of your friend, of your enemy say nothing.
Even the most timid man can deliver a bold speech.
Speak well of the dead.
Speak that I may see thee.
Speaking without thinking, is shooting without aiming.
A soft speech has its poison.
More have repented speech than silence.
Say well or be still.
Let your speech be always with grace, seasoned with salt.
Much speaking and lying are cousins.
Out of the abundance of heart the mouth speaketh (*Matt.*).
It is better to guard speech than to guard wealth.
First think and then speak.
Speech is a mirror of the soul.
Hear much, speak little.
Speak after the manner of men (*Romans*).
If you have no money in your pot have some in your mouth.
He cannot speak well that cannot hold his tongue.
Speak what you will, bad men will turn it ill.
He that speaks much is much mistaken.
The man is wise who speaks few things.
Discretion of speech is more than eloquence.
A man's character is revealed by his speech.
Speak little and to the purpose.
He who speaks sows; who listens reaps.

SPEND:
>Spend and God shall send, spare and ever bare.
>Easy come, easy go.
>To spend much and gain little is the same road to ruin.
>He who more than he is worth doth spend, makes a rope his life to end.

SPIRIT:
>The spirit illuminates every thing.
>The spirit indeed is willing, but the flesh is weak (*Matt.*).

SPIT:
>Spit not into the well where water you may have to drink.
>Who spits against the wind, it fouls his beard.
>He who spits above himself will have it all in his face.

SPORT:
>Sport is sweetest when there are no spectators.

SPOT:
>A spot is most seen on the finest cloth.
>Point not at another's spots with a foul finger.

SPRING:
>In the spring, a young man's fancy lightly turns to thoughts of love (*Tennyson*).

SPY:
>Spies are the ears and eyes of princes.
>The life of a spy is to know, not to be known.

STARS:
>I believe a leaf of grass is no less than the journey work of the stars (*Whitman*).
>The stars rule men, but God rules the stars.

STATE:
>The foundation of a state is its education of its youth.
>Better one suffer than a nation grieve.

STEAL:
>Stop he that will steal a pin, for he will steal an ox.
>Stolen fruit is sweetest.
>He who steals once is never to be trusted.

STEP:
>Step after step the ladder is ascended.

STEP-MOTHER:
>A step-mother has a hard hand.

STITCH:
>A stitch in time saves nine.

STOMACH:
    He whose belly is full believes not him who is fasting.
    The stomach is easier filled than the eye.

STONE:
    Beware of the stone you stumbled at before.
    The stone sharpens knives, but is full itself.
    To kill two birds with one stone.

STORM:
    A good pilot is best tried in a storm.
    Vows made in storms are forgotten in calms.

STRAIGHT:
    Straight trees have crooked roots.

STRANGER:
    Be not forgetful to entertain strangers, for thereby some have entertained angels unaware (*Heb.*).
    In thy company of strangers silence is safe.

STRAW:
    Straws show which way the wind blows.

STRENGTH:
    They that wait upon the Lord shall renew their strength (*Is.*).
    As thy days so shall thy strength be.
    It is excellent to have a giant's strength, but it is tyranny to use it like a giant (*Shakespeare*).
    Brute strength without reason falls of its own weight.
    Let your strength be the law of justice (*Apoc.*).

STUDY:
    I would live to study, not study to live (*Bacon*).

STRETCH:
    Stretch your legs according to your quilt.

STRIKE:
    Many strokes fell great oaks.
    Strike while the iron is hot.

STRONG:
    The strong one is always right.

STUPID:
    Nature delights in punishing stupid people (*Emerson*).
    There is no sin but stupidity (*O. Wilde*).

SUCCESS:
    Success is a ladder which cannot be climbed with your hands in your pockets.

Success comes in a thousand ways but only one kind abideth, that which is built on hard work, wise play and real prayer.
Success makes a fool seem wise.
Success is the reward of toil.
Success has brought many to destruction.
A successful man loses no reputation.

SUFFER:
He who suffers much will know much.
Suffer in order to know, toil in order to have.
The sufferer becomes a chatterer.

SUGAR:
Even sugar itself may spoil a good dish.

SUICIDE:
He dies twice who perishes by his own hand.
It is more brave to live than to die.
He is a coward who commits suicide.

SUMMER:
Do what we can, summer will have its flies.

SUN:
The sun shines on rich and poor alike.

SUNSHINE:
Keep your face always toward the sunshine, and the shadows will fall behind you (*Whitman*).

SUPERSTITION:
A superstition is a premature explanation that overstays its time.
Superstition is the religion of feeble minds.
Superstition poisons and destroys all peace of mind.

SUPPER:
He that steals an old man's supper does him a kindness.
Take a walk after supper.

SURGEON:
A good surgeon must have an eagle's eye, a lady's hand, and a lion's heart.
Tender surgeons make foul wounds.

SUSPICION:
At the gate when suspicion enters love goes out.
Suspicion is the poison of friendship.
Suspicion is the companion of mean souls (*Thomas Paine*).

SWALLOW:
One swallow does not make a summer.

SWEAR:
: He that tells the truth saves himself the trouble of swearing.
: He that swears falsely denies God.
: He that will swear will die.

SWEEP:
: If each one sweeps before his own door, the whole street is clean.

SWEET:
: Sweets to the sweet.
: Take the sweet with the sour.

SWIM:
: The best swimmers are often drowned.

SWORD:
: They that take the sword, shall perish with the sword (*Matt.*).
: Better die with the sword than by the sword.
: One sword keeps another in sheath.
: Use not the sword against him who asks forgiveness.
: He that plays with the sword plays with the devil.

SYMPATHY:
: Rejoice with him that do rejoice, and weep with him that do weep (*Rom.*).
: Our sympathy is cold to the relation of distant misery.
: A brother's suffering claims a brother's pity.

SYSTEM:
: A place for everything and everything in its place.

T

TABLE:
: The table robs more than the thief.
: At a round table there is no dispute of place.

TAILOR:
: There is little to sew where tailors are true.
: A hundred tailors, a hundred weavers, and a hundred millers make three hundred thieves.

TAKE:
: Take things always by the smooth handle.
: Who likes to take hates to give.

TALE:
: A tale twice told, is cabbage twice old.
: Believe not every tale.

TALENT:
: Hide not your talents, they for use were made.

TALK:
- Talk often but never long.
- He that talks to himself speaks to a fool.
- The noisiest drum has nothing in it but air.
- He that knows not how to hold his tongue knows not how to talk.
- Talk does not cook rice (*Chinese*).
- They always talk who never think (*Prov.*).
- To talk without thinking is to shoot without aiming.
- The greatest talkers, the least doers.
- Much bruit, little fruit.
- The talker sows, the listener reaps.
- The less people think the more they talk.
- Two great talkers will not travel together.
- The noisy fowler catches no birds.
- Great talkers are commonly liars.
- A great talker is a great liar.
- A man of words and not of deeds, is like a garden full of weeds.
- Great talkers are like leaky pitchers, everything runs out of them.

TASTE:
- Whether sugar be white or red, it preserves its proper taste.
- Taste is the literary conscience of the soul (*Joubert*).

TAXES:
- In this world nothing is certain but death and taxes (*Franklin*).

TEA:
- Love and scandal are the best sweetener of tea.

TEACH:
- Better untaught than ill taught.
- He teacheth ill who teacheth all.
- Who teaches often learns himself.
- I don't teach, I only tell (*Montaigne*).
- A teacher should be sparing of his smiles.

TEARS:
- Tears are the noble language of the eye.
- The fewer his years, the fewer his tears.
- Woman's weapons, water drops (*Shelley*).
- Only human eyes can weep.
- Tears are the silent language of grief.
- Nothing dries so fast as a woman's tears.
- In tears was I born, and after tears I die (*Greek*).
- Onion tears do not touch the heart.
- Women laugh when they can and weep when they will.

Onions can make even heirs and widows weep.
A small tear relieves a great sorrow.
TELL:
Don't tell everything you know.
TEMPER:
To a boiling pot flies come not.
TEMPERANCE:
Temperance is the best medicine.
TEMPLE:
The truest temples are fixed in the heart.
TEMPTATION:
He who avoids temptation avoids the sin.
An open box tempts an honest man.
May God defend me from myself.
Lead us not into temptation, but deliver us from sin (*Matt.*).
Watch and pray, that ye enter not into temptation (*Matt.*).
Blessed is the man that endureth temptation (*James*).
TEST:
The proof of gold is fire, the proof of woman, gold, the proof of man, a woman.
THIEF:
A thief thinks every man steals.
All are not thieves that dogs bark at.
He that shows his purse bribes the thief.
Set a thief to catch a thief.
When it thunders a thief becomes honest.
A thief knows a thief as a wolf knows a wolf.
The thief is frightened even by a mouse.
If you would make a thief honest trust him.
We hang little thieves and take off our hats to great ones.
He that will steal an egg will steal an ox.
Great thieves hang little ones.
THINGS:
Things that are worst will sometimes mend.
THINKING:
Great minds think alike.
THIRST:
Who has no thirst has no business at the fountain.
THISTLES:
Thistles are salad for asses.

THORN:
   Without thorns, no roses.
THOROUGHNESS:
   Never do things by halves.
   Thoroughness is the most difficult habit to acquire but it is the pearl of great price, worth all the worry and trouble of the search (Oster).
THOUGHT:
   Think today and speak tomorrow.
   I pray thee God that I may be beautiful within.
   Think much, speak little, and write less.
   Great thoughts reduced to practice become great acts.
   Second thoughts are wisest.
   He thinks not well that thinks not again.
   There is nothing either good or bad, but thinking makes it so (Shakespeare).
   He is a fool that thinks not that another thinks.
   To live is to think.
   A wise man's thoughts walk within him, but a fool's without him.
   Our thoughts are often worse than we are.
   To think is to converse with one's self.
   Thought is free.
   As he thinketh in his heart, so is he (Prov.).
   Good thoughts, even if forgotten, do not perish.
   He is never alone that is accompanied with noble thoughts.
   Men suffer from thinking more than from anything else (Tolstoy).
   A moment's thinking is an hour of words.
THREAD:
   The thread breaks where it is thinnest.
THREAT:
   Threat without power, are like powder without ball.
   Barking dogs never bite.
   Who threatens warns.
   Dogs bark and caravans pass.
   His bark is worse than his bite.
THRIFT:
   A shilling spent idly by a fool may be picked up by a wiser man.
   Wise men say keep somewhat till a rainy day.
   Who more than he is worth doth spend, he makes a rope his life to end.
   Take care of the pence and the pounds will take care of themselves.

Penny and penny laid up will be many.
Of saving cometh having.
He that thrive, must rise at five. He that hath thriven, may lie till seven.
If you keep a thing for seven years, you are sure to find a use for it at last.
If you put nothing into your purse, you can take nothing out.
It is too late to spare, when the bottom is bare.

TIME:
Make use of time if you have eternity.
Time is God's, not ours.
Use time as though you knew its value.
An inch of time cannot be bought by an inch of gold.
Lost time is not found again.
There is a time to fish and a time to dry nets.
Every scrap of a wise man's time is worth saving.
A mouse may cut a cable in time.
There is a time for all things.
To things immortal, time can do no wrong.
The greatest sacrifice is the sacrifice of time.
A stitch in time saves nine.
Nothing is so dear and precious like time.
When you have come through a bad time, to tell of it takes the thorn out (Mary Webb).
Time heals sorrow.
Man cannot buy time.
In time even a bear can learn to dance.
Father Time lays his hand lightly on those who have used him well (Dickens).
Time is money.

TIMES:
Other times, other manners.

TIMID:
Bashfulness is an ornament in youth but a reproach to old age.
Timidity is an enemy to poverty.
The timid sees dangers which do not exist.

TIRED:
Tired folks are quarrelsome.

TITLES:
Empty heads love long titles.

TOBACCO:
Tobacco "hic" if a man be well it will make him sick.

TODAY:
One today is worth two tomorrows.
Today a man in gold, tomorrow closed in clay.
Today at good cheer, tomorrow on the bier.
Today is yesterday's pupil.

TOIL:
He who toils with pain will eat pleasure.
Toil is a prayer.
Nothing is achieved without toil.

TOMORROW:
Tomorrow, tomorrow, not today, hear the people say; never put off till tomorrow, what you can do today.
Boast not thyself of tomorrow, for thou knowest not what a day may bring forth (*Prov.*).

TONGUE:
Thistles and thorns prick sore, but evil tongue prick more.
He that knows not how to hold his tongue, knows not how to talk.
An ox is taken by the horns, and a man by the tongue.
A still tongue makes a wise head.
A good tongue is a good weapon.
Keep not two tongues in one mouth.
The tongue can no man tame.
Keep thy tongue from evil and thy lips from speaking guile.
A man's tongue sometimes leads him to the gallows.
He who holds his tongue saves his head.
The tongue of a bad friend cuts more than a knife.
Train your tongue to say, I do not know; lest thou be entrapped into falsehood.
What among men is good and bad, the tongue.
Birds are entangled by their feet, and men by their tongues.
Confine your tongue, lest it confine you.
One tongue is enough for two women.
The tongue speaks wisely when the soul is wise.
The tongue is a sharper weapon than the sword.
Let not your tongue outrun your thought.
The wise man's tongue is a shield, not a sword.
Turn your tongue seven times before speaking.
The tongue is not steel, yet it cuts.

TRADE:
> He that brings not up his son to some trade makes him a thief.
> He who has a trade may travel through the world.
> The first article a young trader offers for sale is honesty.

TRADESMAN:
> A tradesman who cannot lie may shut up his shop.

TRAINING:
> Train up a child in the way he should go (*Prov.*).

TRAVEL:
> Travel makes a wise man better, but a fool worse.
> Travel teaches toleration.
> A fool wanders, the wise man travels.
> He that travels much knows much.
> Leave thy house, O youth, and seek out alien shores.

TREACHERY:
> Treachery in the end destroys itself.
> Betrayers are hated by those whom they benefit.
> He covers me with his wings and bites me with his bill.

TREASON:
> A traitor is a coward.
> No religion binds men to be traitors.

TREE:
> The tree is known by his fruits (*Matt.*).
> When the tree falls the shade is gone.
> Good fruit never comes from a bad tree.
> When the tree is fallen all go with their hatchets.

TRIALS:
> Trials teach us what we are; they dig up the soil and let us see what we are made of (*Spurgeon*).

TRIFLE:
> Little drops of water, little grains of sand, make the mighty ocean and the peasant sand (*Carney*).

TROUBLE:
> Forgetting trouble is the way to cure it.
> Never trouble trouble till trouble troubles you.

TRUST:
> In God is our trust.
> If you trust before you try, you may repent before you die.
> Eat a peck of salt with a man before you trust him.
> Put your trust in God, but keep your powder dry (*Cromwell*).
> From those I trust God guard me, from those I mistrust, I will guard myself.

TRUTH:
>Better suffer for truth than prosper by falsehoods.
>A lie travels round the world while truth is putting on her boots.
>Oil and truth will come to the surface.
>Every man seeks for truth, but God only knows who has found it.
>Be so true to thyself as thou be not false to others (*Bacon*).
>Children and fools speak true.
>Truth is the highest thing that man may keep (*Chaucer*).
>All truths are not to be told.
>A truth-teller finds the door closed against him.
>Truth crushed to earth shall ripen again (*Bryant*).
>Truth never hurts the teller.
>Truth hath a quiet breast.
>Truth needs no memory.
>Truth is often eclipsed but never extinguished.
>Plato is dear to me, but dearer still is the truth (*Greek*).
>Truth makes the devil blush.

TRY:
>If at first you don't succeed, try, try again.
>Try the ice before you venture on it.

TWO:
>Two watermelons cannot be held in one hand.
>Two heads are better than one.

TYRANT:
>Resistance to a tyrant is obedience to God (*Jefferson*).
>When law ends tyranny begins.
>Happy the tyrant who dies in bed.

U

UGLY:
>No one blames a man for being ugly.

UNATTAINABLE:
>Foxes, when they cannot reach the grapes, say they are sour.

UNCERTAINTY:
>All between the cradle and the coffin is uncertain.
>Between the hand and the lip the morsel may slip.

UNDER-DOG:
>He that is down, down with him, cried the world.
>Men shut their doors against a setting sun.
>The conquered is never wise.
>When the ox falls, many sharpen their knives.

UNDERSTANDING:
    Understanding is the faculty of reflection.
    With all thy getting, get understanding (Prov.).
    Give I an understanding, but no tongue (Shakespeare).

UNITY:
    He that is not with me is against me (Matt.).
    Behold, how good and how pleasant it is for brethren to dwell together in unity (Ps.).
    We must all hang together or we shall all hang separately (Franklin).
    Weak things united become strong.
    The lone sheep is in danger of the wolf.
    United we stand, divided we fall (Morris).
    Union gives strength to the humble.

UNIVERSITY:
    A university is a place where the pebbles are polished and diamonds are dimmed (Ingersoll).
    Alma Mater (Fostering mother).

UNKINDNESS:
    Unkindness has no remedy at law.
    A wise man cares not for what he cannot have.

UNLUCKY:
    If I raised soup, I'd have a fork instead of a spoon.
    He falls on his back and breaks his nose.

UNRESTRAINED:
    The vessel that will not obey the helm will have to obey the rocks.

UNSOCIABILITY:
    Who eats his cock alone must saddle his horse alone.

UNWELCOME:
    As unwelcome as water in a ship.
    As welcome as rain in the spring.

UNWILLINGNESS:
    Nothing is easy to the unwilling.

UPRIGHT:
    An empty bag cannot stand upright.

USE:
    The used key is always bright.
    A used plough shines, standing water stinks.
    He who is of no use to himself, is of no use to any one else.
    Nothing is useless to a man of sense.

USEFUL:
    Unless what we do is useful, glory is in vain.
USELESS:
    Nothing is useless to a person of sense.
USURY:
    To borrow on usury brings sudden beggary.

V

VAINGLORY:
    Vainglory blossoms but never bears.
VALOUR:
    In valour there is hope.
    Valour flourishes by a wound.
VANITY:
    Vanity of vanities, all is vanity (*Eccl.*).
    An ounce of vanity spoils a hundred weight of merit.
    Vanity is the sixth sense.
    Vanity is the food of fools.
VARNISHING:
    Varnishing hides a crack.
VENGEANCE:
    The noblest vengeance is to forgive.
VENTURING:
    Don't carry all your eggs in one basket.
    Dry shoes won't catch fish.
    Hang not all your bells on one horse.
    Nothing ventured, nothing gained.
    Try the ice before you venture on it.
VICE:
    Our pleasant vices are made the whip to scourge us (*Shakespeare*).
    He who plunges into vice is like one who rolls from the top of a precipice (*Chinese*).
    One vice begets another.
    Great vices as well as great virtues make men famous.
    Every vice fights against nature.
    Where vice is, vengeance follows.
    Search others for their virtues, yourself for your vices.
    Vices creep into our hearts under the name of virtues.
    We make a ladder of our vices, if we trample them underfoot (*St. Augustine*).
    After one vice a greater follows.

VICTORY:
- To who God will, there be victory.
- He conquers twice who upon victory conquers himself.
- There are some defeats more triumphant than victories.
- It is a great victory that comes without blood.

VIRTUE:
- Beauty is the flower, but virtue is the fruit of life.
- Virtue unites man with God.
- Virtue is a jewel of great price.
- Virtue is the first title of nobility.
- Virtue and vice cannot live under the same roof.
- He who dies for virtue does not perish.
- I wrap myself in my virtue.
- Virtue and a trade are the best portion for children.
- Virtue lives beyond the grave.
- Poverty does not destroy virtue, nor wealth destroy it.
- Virtue and happiness are mother and daughter.
- Virtue is the health of the soul.
- With virtue one may conquer the world.
- Virtue even in rags will keep warm.
- The virtue of a man must be judged not only by his acts but from his intentions (*Democritus*).

VISIT:
- Visits should be short, like a winter's day.
- Lest you are too troublesome, hasten away.
- Friendship increases in visiting friends, but more in visiting them seldom.
- Friends are lost by calling often and calling seldom.

VOWS:
- Men's vows are women's traitors (*Shakespeare*).
- Vows are made in storms and forgotten in calm.
- Her voice was ever soft, gentle, and low, an excellent thing in a woman.

VULGAR:
- Vulgarity defiles fine garments more than mud.

W

WAGES:
- Men work but slowly that have poor wages.

WAIT:
    Wait is a hard word to the hungry.
    Everything comes to those who can wait.

WALKING:
    It is good to walk until the blood appear on the cheek, but not the sweat on the brow.

WALLS:
    Walls have ears.
    A white wall is the fool's paper.

WANT:
    The more one has the more one wants.
    When we want, friends are scarce.
    There is no woe like to want.

WAR:
    A just war is better than unjust peace.
    He that preaches war is the devil's chaplain.
    The first blow is as much as two.
    There never was a good war, nor a bad peace.
    War is death's feast.
    War is the child of pride.
    Wars bring scars.
    To be prepared for war is one of the most effective means of preserving peace (George Washington).
    In war it is not permitted to make a mistake twice.
    A wise man should try everything before resorting to war.
    War makes thieves, and peace hangs them.
    Dying is more honourable than killing (Seneca).
    Wars are pleasant in the ear, not in the eye.
    War is sweet to those who have not experienced it.
    Wars, hateful to mothers (Horace).
    When drums speak, law is silent.
    Talk of the war, but do not go to it.

WASH:
    You can wash only the body, but not the soul.

WASTE:
    Waste brings woe.
    Wilful waste brings woeful want.

WATCHING:
    A watched pan is long in boiling.

WATER:
    We never know the worth of water till the well is dry.
    Sweet water cannot flow from a foul spring.

WEAK:
    Every man has a weak side.
    Weak men had need to be witty.
    In a just cause the weak overcomes the strong.

WEALTH:
    Men make wealth, and women preserve it.
    A little house well filled, a little land well tilled, and a little wife well willed are great riches.
    Ill gather, ill spent.
    A great fortune in the hands of a fool is a great misfortune.
    A good wife and health are a man's best wealth.
    He who multiplies riches multiplies cares.
    The greatest wealth is contentment with a little.
    Wealth conquered Rome after Rome had conquered the world.
    He is rich enough that wants nothing.
    Wealth is not his that has it, but his that enjoys it.
    Of lawful wealth the devil takes the half, of unlawful, the whole, and the owners, too.

WEAPON:
    A weapon is an enemy even to its owner.

WEAR:
    It is better to wear out than to rust out.

WEATHER:
    After clouds, clear sun.
    Winter weather and women's thoughts often change.
    The evening red, and the morning gray, is the sign of a fair day.

WEDDING:
    Winter and wedlock lames man and beast.

WEED:
    No garden without weeds.

WEEP:
    When the vulture dies the hen does not weep.
    He who loves you well makes you weep.
    Better children weep than old men.
    Better the cottage where one is merry than the palace where one weeps.

WEIGHT:
    Weigh justly and sell dearly.
    Good weight and measure is heaven's treasure.
WELCOME:
    Who comes seldom is welcome, as welcome as flower in May.
    They are welcome that bring.
WELL (NOUN):
    Don't throw a stone into a well from which you have drunk.
    When the well is dry we know the worth of water.
WELL (ADV.):
    All is well that ends well.
WELL-DOING:
    He teaches me to be good that does me good.
    Never be weary of well doing.
    Well is good, but to do well is better.
    Say well and do well and with one letter; say well is good, but do well is better.
    He that would do no ill, must do all good or sit still.
WHISPER:
    He that doth good for praise only, meriteth but a puff of wind.
    The whisperer's tongue is worse than the serpent's tooth.
    Where there is whispering there is lying.
WICKED:
    A wicked heart fears God when it thunders.
    A wicked man is afraid of his own memory.
    The triumphing of the wicked is short (*Prov.*).
    A wicked man is his own hell.
    There is no peace unto the wicked.
    Ye have ploughed wickedness, ye have reaped iniquity (*Hosea*).
    An ill man is worst when he appeareth good.
    A picked companion invites all to go to hell.
    Never was the wicked wise.
    The rotten apple injures its neighbors.
    The wicked ears are deaf to wisdom's call.
    The wicked heart never fears God but when it thunders.
    Wicked men cannot be friends.
    No man ever becomes wicked all at once.
    He who brings aid to the wicked grieves for it later.
    The sun shines even on the wicked.
WIDOW:
    The rich widow cries with one eye and laughs with the other.

WIFE:

A good wife and a good name, hath no mate in goods and fame.
He that has a wife and children must not sit with his fingers in his mouth.
A good wife and health, are man's best wealth.
A prudent wife is from the Lord (Prov.).
A virtuous woman is a crown to her husband (Prov.).
She looketh well to the ways of her husband and eateth not the bread of idleness (Prov.).
Giving honor unto the wife as the weaker vessel (Prov.).
It is not good that man should be alone.
Saith Solomon the wise, a good wife is a good prize.
A cheerful wife is the joy of life.
A man's best fortune or his worst is a wife.
A wife is not to be chosen by the eye only.
An expensive wife, makes a pensive husband.
An obedient wife commands her husband.
Choose a house made and a wife to make.
Choose a wife rather by your ear than by your eye.
Discreet wives have neither eyes nor ears.
He knows little who will tell his wife all he knows.
He that has a wife has strife.
He that has a wife has a master.
A fair wife without a fortune, is a fine house without furniture.
Go down the ladder when thou married a wife, go up when thou choosest a friend.
It is a good horse that never stumbles, and a good wife that never grumbles.
Man's best possession is a loving wife.
The calmest husbands make the stormiest wives.
The wife that expects to have a good name, is always at home, as if she were lame.
The wife that loves the looking-glass hates the saucepan.
Wives may be merry and honest too (Shakespeare).
Wives must be had, whether good or bad.
Empty rooms make giddy housewives.
Let not the hen talk and the cock be silent.
Man has found remedies against all poisonous creatures, but none was yet found against a bad wife.
A bad wife is the shipwreck of her husband.
A poor man who takes a rich wife has a ruler, not a wife.

The bitterest morsel of human life is a bad wife.
A good wife is a good gift.
If the wife sins, the husband is not innocent.
A virtuous wife rules her husband by obeying him.
Choose neither a wife nor linen by candle-light.
Every married man should think his wife the one good woman in the world.
He who does not honor his wife dishonours himself.
Fire, water, and a bad wife are three great evils.
No fellow is so poor that he has not a wife on his arm.

WILLINGNESS:
All things are easy that are done willingly.
Nothing is impossible to a willing heart.
Where there is a will there is a way.
A willing mind makes a light foot.

WINE:
When wine enters, modesty departs.
When wine sinks, words swim.
Wine makes all sorts of creatures at table.
Wine turns a man inside outside.
Wine has drowned more than the sea.
Wine in excess keeps neither secrets nor promises.
Wine in, wit out.

WISDOM:
The price of wisdom is above rubies (*Job*).
What is not wisdom is danger.
The wisdom of the world is foolishness with God (*I Cor.*).
Wisdom giveth life to them that have it.
An ounce of wisdom is worth a pound of wit.
Wisdom to a poor man is a diamond set in lead.
A flow of words is no proof of wisdom.
Wisdom is best taught by distress.
In wisdom's ranks he stands, the just who stands prepared to meet the worst.
Learn wisdom by the follies of others.
Wisdom and goodness to the vile seems vile (*Shakespeare*).
Wisdom is not finally tested in schools.
Wisdom is the wealth of the wise.
Man's chief wisdom consists in knowing his follies.
Wisdom is the mother of all acts.

In youth and beauty wisdom is but rare (Homer).
That man is wisest who realizes that his wisdom is worthless (Socrates).

WISE:
Be ye therefore wise as serpents, and harmless as doves (Matt.).
Woe unto them that are wise in their own eyes and prudent in their own sight (Ps.).
A wise man may sometimes take counsel of a fool.
A word to the wise is sufficient.
Where one is wise two are happy.
All countries are a wise man's home.
He is wise enough that can keep himself warm.
It is easy to be wise after the event.
Oftentimes to please fools wise men err.
The wise man is he who does not think he is so.
The wise learn many things from their foes.
You may be a wise man though you cannot make a watch.
How cautious are the wise (Homer).
The wise man must carry the fool on his shoulder.
It takes a wise man to be recognized a wise man.
Wise men have their mouths in their hearts; fools their hearts in their mouths.
Who consorts with the wise will become wise.
No man is wise enough by himself.
The wise man may look ridiculous in the company of fools.
If things were to be done twice, all would be wise.
Many talk like philosophers and act like fools.
The wise man, even when he holds his tongue, says more than the fool when he speaks.

WISH:
You can't get rich by wishing.
Wishes can never fill a sack.
Mere wishes are silly fishes.

WIT:
An ounce of wit is worth a pound of sorrow.
The more wit, the less courage.
Wit and wisdom are born with a man.
Wit without wisdom cuts other men's meat and its own fingers.

WOLF:
The death of the wolf is the breath of the sheep.
Wake not a sleeping wolf.

The wolf may lose his teeth, but never his nature.
The wolf finds reason for taking the lamb.

WOMAN:
Silence gives grace to a woman.
Women are ships and must be manned.
A virtuous woman is a crown to her husband (*Prov.*).
Bad words make women worse.
The tongue of women is their sword, and they take care not to let it rust.
A woman's mind and winter's wind change oft.
Silence is the best armament for a woman.
The happiest women, like the happiest nations, have no history.
A good woman is worth, if she were sold, the fairest crown, that is made of pure gold.
Women and elephants never forget.
A woman's counsel is sometimes good.
Women were created for the comfort of men.
Women, wind and fortune are ever changing.
A woman and a melon are hard to choose.
With women one should never venture to joke.
A woman and a glass are even in danger.
Women laugh when they can and weep when they will.
Between a woman's "yes and no," there is not room for a pin to go.

WONDER:
Wonder is the daughter of ignorance.
Wonder is the first class of philosophy (*Aristotle*).

WOOD:
He that fears leaves let him not go into the wood.

WORD:
Better one word in time than two afterwards.
By thy words thou shalt be condemned.
He that hath knowledge spareth his words (*Prov.*).
From words to deeds is a great space.
Without knowing the force of words; it is impossible to know men (*Confucius*).
One ill word asketh another.
A man's word is his honour.
A word before is worth two after.
Take a horse by his bridle and a man by his word.
Few words are best.
A good word costs no more than bad one.

Cool words scald not the tongue.
A man of words and not of deeds, is like a garden full of weeds.
A word hurts more than a wound.
Good words cost no more than bad.
A kind word leads the cow into the stable.
Few words many deeds.
A word spoken is an arrow let fly.
Evening words are not like to morning.
Good words cost nothing, but are worth much.
Good words cool more than cool water.
Good words without deeds, are bushes and weeds.
Great talkers are never great doers.
Soft words win hard hearts.
A good word for a bad one is worth much, and costs little.
When the word is out it belongs to another.
Soft words hurt not the mouth.
Prove your words, by your deeds.
Words should be weighed not counted.
Saying and doing have quarrelled and parted.

WORK:
A work ill done must be done twice (*I Cor.*).
Every man's work shall be made manifest.
If any should not work, neither should he eat (*II Thess.*).
All work and no play makes John a dull boy.
Never was good work done without much trouble.
No pains, no gains; no sweat, no sweet.
Slow work produces fine goods.
There is no substitute for hard work (*Edison*).
The result tests the work (*Washington*).
Where there are too many, there is little work.
He that will not endure labour in this world, had better not be born.
To labour is to pray.
No bees, no honey; no work, no money.
The better workman, the better husband.
Work consists of whatever a body is obliged to do (*Mark Twain*)
Every one should be judged by his works.
Work has better root, but sweet fruits.
There is no substitute for hard work (*Edison*).
A work well begun, is well done.
Work is not disgrace, the disgrace is idleness.

When I die, may I be taken in the midst of work (*Ovid*).
To labour is to pray.
A good carpenter does not complain of his tools.
An ill workman quarrels with his tools.
He who has money to throw away, let him employ workers, and not stand by.

WORKERS:
A lot of today's trouble arises from workers who don't think and thinkers who don't work.

WORLD:
A man may know the world without leaving his own home.
Be wisely worldly, but not worldly wise.
The world is a fine place and worth fighting for (*Hemingway*).
The world is as you take it.
The world is a prophecy of worlds to come.
The world is a ladder for some to go up and some down.
The world is a bride superbly dressed, who weds for dowry must pay his soul (*Hafiz*).

WORRY:
Worry is the interest we pay on trouble before it is due.
Nothing in the affairs of men is worthy of great anxiety.
Worry less, play more, drink less, breathe well, ride less, walk more, frown less, smile more.

WORSHIP:
For when two or three are gathered together in my name, there am I in the middle of them (*Matt.*).
They that worship God merely from fear, would worship the devil too if he appear.
There may be worshipping without words.

WORST:
Things at their worst will mend.
It is best to know the worst at once.

WORTH:
So much is a man worth as he esteems himself.
All good things are cheap, all bad are very dear.
Worth may be blamed but never shamed.

WOUND:
The wound that bleedeth inwardly is the most dangerous.
A wound heals but the scar remains.
The knife wound heals, the tongue never.

WRITING:
　Either write things worth reading or do things worth writing (*Franklin*).
　What comes from the heart goes to the heart.

WRONG:
　Better suffer than do ill.
　No wrong without remedy.
　He who does the wrong forgets it, but not he who receives it.
　The silent man still suffers long.

Y

YEARS:
　The more thy years, the nearer thy grave.
　The year doth nothing else but open and shut.
　Each passing year robs us of something.
　Nothing is swifter than the year.
　Give us years—troubles come of themselves.
　The years of a man's life pass like a dream.
　Years know more than the books.

YOUTH:
　Remember thy creator in the days of thy youth (*Eccl.*).
　The days of our youth are the days of our glory (*Byron*).
　The majority of men employ the first portion of their life in making the other portion miserable.
　Youth is drunkenness without wine (*Goethe*).
　The wildest colts make the best horses.
　While the morning shines gather the flowers.
　Our youth will build the future on the foundation we lay today.

Z

ZEAL:
　It is good to be zealously affected always in a good thing (*Gal.*).
　Zeal is like fire; it wants both feeding and watching.
　Zeal without knowledge is a fire without a light.
　Zeal without knowledge is folly.

Part III

Selected Quotations

1. Give us grace and strength to forbear and to persevere. Give us courage and gaiety and the quiet mind, spare to us our friends, soften to us our enemies. (*On bronze in St. Giles Cathedral, Edinburgh.*)
2. "What is the use of this new invention?" someone asked Franklin. "What is the use of a newborn child," was the answer.
3. "Little deeds of kindness, little words of love,
   Help to make earth happy like the heaven above." (*Carney*)
4. I have travelled many countries, but I have never met a man I didn't like.
5. This life is not the book; it is only the first chapter of the book. (*Morrison*)
6. The end of birth is death; the end of death is birth—this is ordained. (*Arnold*)
7. Life is real; life is earnest!
   And the grave is not its goal.
   Dust thou art, to dust returneth,
   Was not spoken of the soul. (*Longfellow*)
8. If you want knowledge, you must toil for it, and if pleasure you must toil for it. Toil is the law. Pleasure comes through toil, and not by self-indulgence and indolence. When one gets to love work, his life is a happy one. (*Ruskin*)
9. "God looks not to see if the hands are full;
   He looks to see if they are clean."
10. Whether you be a man or woman, you will never do anything in the world without courage. It is the greatest quality of the mind, next to honor. (*Allen*)
11. "The good we can each of us accomplish in this world is small. The good that all men in all ages could accomplish if they would, is vast. But in order that this may be done, each working being must serve his own generation, and do his part to render the next generation more efficient." (*Woolsey*)

12. "Working is praying," said one of the holiest of men. And he spoke the truth. If a man will but do his work from a sense of duty, which is for the sake of God. (*Kingsley*)
13. "A man must stand erect, not be kept erect by others."
14. He who would have full power must first strive to get power over his own mind. (*King Alfred*)
15. It is nothing for a man to hold up his head in a calm; but to maintain his post when all others have quitted their ground, and there to stand upright where all other men are beaten down. This is divine and praiseworthy. (*Seneca*)
16. Let man aim at the good which belongs to him. What is this good? A mind reformed and pure, the imitator of God raising itself above things human, confining all its desires within itself. (*Seneca*)
17. Riches ... the greatest source of human trouble. (*Seneca*)
18. He is a high-souled man who sees riches spread around him, and hears rather than feels that they are his. It is much not to be corrupted by fellowship with riches. Great is he who in the midst of wealth is poor, but safer he who has no wealth at all. (*Seneca*)
19. While we are among men let us cultivate kindness: let us not be to any man a cause either of peril or of fear. (*Seneca*)
20. Let him who hath conferred a favor hold his tongue. In conferring a favor nothing should be more avoided than pride. (*Seneca*)
21. How many are unworthy of the light? and yet the day dawns. (*Seneca*)
22. Think of God oftener than your breath. Let discourse of God be renewed daily more surely than your food. (*Epictetus*)
23. When Archelaus sent a message to Socrates to express the intention of making him rich, Socrates bade the messenger inform him that at Athena four quarts of meal might be bought for three halfpence, and the foundation flow with water.
24. The well-being of our souls depends only on what we are; and nobleness of character is nothing else but steady love of good and steady scorn of evil. (*Epictetus*)
25. Happiness may fly away, pleasure cease to be obtainable, wealth decay, friends fail or prove unkind: but the power to serve God never fails, and the love of Him is never rejected. (*Epictetus*)
26. Thaler, when asked what was the commonest of all possessions, answered: "Hope; for even those who have nothing else have hope."

27. When we were children, our parents entrusted us to a tutor who kept a continual watch that we might not suffer harm; but, when we grow to manhood, God hands us over to an inborn conscience to guard us. We must, therefore, by no means despise this guardianship, since in that case we shall both be displeasing to God and enemies to our own conscience. (*Epictetus*)
28. "Will you walk in my parlor:" said the spider to the fly; "'Tis the prettiest little parlor that ever you did spy."
29. Lost yesterday, somewhere between sunrise and sunset, two golden hours, each set with sixty diamond minutes. No reward is offered for they are gone forever.
30. I pray the prayer of Plato old: God make thee beautiful within.
31. Philanthropy is almost the only virtue which is sufficiently appreciated by mankind. (*Thearon*)
32. The grave itself is but a covered bridge leading from light to light through a brief darkness.
33. Do not pray for easy lives. Pray to be stronger men! Do not pray for tasks equal to your powers. Pray for powers equal to your tasks. (*Brooks*)
34. There must be not a balance of power, but a community of power; not organized rivalries, but an organized common peace. (*Woodrow Wilson*)
35. The man I know not for I am not acquainted with his mind. (*Diogenes*)
36. Remember this—that very little is needed to make a happy life. (*Marcus Aurelius*)
37. Forgiveness is better than punishment; for the one is proof of a gentle, the other of a savage nature. (*Diogenes*)
38. Life has a value only when it has something valuable as its object. (*Hegel*)
39. Be not forgetful of prayer. Every time you pray, if your prayer is sincere, there will be new feeling and new meaning in it which will give you fresh courage; and you will understand that prayer is an education. (*Dostoyevsky*)
40. I believe that in the end the truth will conquer. (*Wycliffe*)
41. The loss of wealth is loss of dirt,
All sages in all times assert. (*Heywood*)
42. Some have too much, yet still do crave;
I little have and seek no more;
They are but poor, though much they have
And I am rich with little store. (*Dyer*)

43. No pleasure is comparable to the standing upon the vantage-ground of truth. (*Bacon*)
44. A mere madness, to live like a witch and die rich. (*Burton*)
45. Under this window in stormy weather
    I marry this man and woman together.
    Let not but Him who rules the thunder
    Put this man and woman asunder. (*Swift*)
46. When you fall into a man's conversation, the first thing you should consider is, whether he has a greater inclination to hear you, or that you should hear him. (*Steele*)
47. Of all the affection which attend human life, the love of glory is the most ardent. (*Steele*)
48. He who says there is no such thing as an honest man, you may be sure is himself a knave. (*Berkeley*)
49. I have taught you, my dear flock, for above thirty years how to live, and I will show you in a very short time how to die. (*Sandys*)
50. Blessed is he who expects nothing, for he shall never be disappointed. (*Pope*)
51. I am a great friend to public amusements, for they keep people from vice.
52. For my part, I'd tell the truth and shame the devil. (*Johnson*)
53. A mother's pride, a father's joy. (*Scott*)
54. I first gave it a dose of castor oil, and then I christened it: so now the poor child is ready for either world. (*Smith*)
55. Whose lives are mottoes of the heart
    Whose truths electrify the sage. (*Campbell*)
56. Who ran to help me when I fell
    And with some pretty story tell
    Or kiss the place to make it well?—my Mother. (*Taylor*)
57. Those who have lost an infant are never, as it were, without an infant child. They are the only persons who, in one sense, retain it always. (*Hunt*)
58. Blood of the martyrs is the seed of the church. (*Tertullian* 160-240 A.D.)
59. Where we love is home
    Home that our feet may leave, but not our hearts. (*Holmes*)
60. A fair little girl sat under a tree
    Sewing as long as her eyes could see;
    Then smoothed her work, and folded it right,
    And said, "Dear work, good night, good night!" (*Lord Houghton*)
61. To strive, to seek, to find and not to yield. (*Inscribed on the*

memorial cross erected to the memory of Captain Robert Scott and his men at Hutt Point in the Antarctic.)

62. He gave people of his best
    His worst he kept, his best he gave.
63. It lies around us like a cloud.
    A world we do not see.
    Yet the sweet closing of an eye
    May bring us there to be.
64. The only reward of virtue is virtue;
    the only way to have a friend is to be one. (Emerson)
65. Look not mournfully in to the past; it comes not back again. Wisely improve the present; it is thine. Go forth to meet the shadowy future, without fear, and with a merry heart. (Translated from German by Longfellow) The original inscription on the wall of the chapel of St. Gilgen, near Salzburg in the Austrian Alps.
66. Why fear death? Death is only a beautiful adventure. (Frohman, 1860-1915. Last words to a group of friends as the Lusitania was sinking, May 7, 1915)
67. Imagination is as good as many voyages—but how much cheaper. (Curtis)
68. Every mother who has lost an infant has gained a child of immortal youth. (Curtis)
69. In life our absent friend is far away;
    But death may bring our friend exceedingly near. (Possetti)
70. Every step is an end, and every step is a fresh beginning. (Goethe)
71. Women and elephants never forget. (Parkes)
72. It is generally better to deal by speech than by letter. (Bacon)
73. Machiavelli says virtue and riches seldom settle on one man.
74. Few men make themselves masters of the things they write or speak. (Selden)
75. Philosophy is nothing but discretion. (Selden)
76. Deceive not thy physician, confessor nor lawyer. (Herbert)
77. Good words are worth much and cost little. (Herbert)
78. By supper more have been killed than Galen ever cured. (Herbert)
79. Stay till the lame messenger comes, if you will know the truth of the thing.
80. Life is half spent before we know what it is. (Herbert)
81. A few honest men are better than numbers; if you choose godly honest men to be captains of horse, honest men will follow them. (Cromwell)

82. Speech was given to the ordinary sort of men whereby to communicate their mind; but to wise men, whereby to conceal it. (South)
83. Teach me to live, that I may dread
    The grave as little as my bed. (Ken)
84. Many a dangerous temptation comes to us in fine gay colors that are but skin-deep. (Henry)
85. All men think all men mortal but themselves. (Parnell)
86. How pleasant is Saturday night
    When I've tried all the week to be good,
    And not spoke a word that was bad,
    And obliged everyone that I could. (Sproat)
87. In every man's writings, the character of the writer must be recorded. (Carlyle)
88. Get up: for when all things are merry and glad
    Good children should never be lazy and sad;
    For God gives us daylight, dear sister, that we
    May rejoice like the lark and may work like the bee. (Lady Hastings)
89. A great city is that which has the greatest men and women. (Whitman)
90. Learn to live and live to learn,
    Ignorance like a fire doth burn,
    Little tasks make large return. (Taylor)
91. Art thou in misery, brother? Then I pray
    Be comforted! Thy grief shall pass away.
    Art thou elated? Ah, be not too gay;
    Temper thy joy: this too shall pass away. (Hayne)
92. Life is my college. May I graduate well and earn some honor. (Alcott)
93. I know what death means—a liberator for her, a teacher for us. (Alcott)
94. A rich man beginning to fall is helped up by his friends; but a poor man being down is thrust also away by his friend. (Apoc.)
95. Whether it be to friend or foe, talk not of other men's lives. (Apoc.)
96. Great is truth and mighty above all things. (Apoc.)
97. Blessed is the man that endureth temptation, for when he is tried, he shall receive the crown of life. (N. T.)
98. Every good gift and every perfect gift is from above. (N. T.)
99. The love of money is the root of all evil. (N. T.)

100. Whom the Lord loveth he chasteneth. (N. T.)
101. Prove all things; hold fast that which is good. (N. T.)
102. Be ye angry and sin not; let not the sun go down upon your wrath. (N. T.)
103. The things which are seen are temporal; but the things which are not seen are eternal. (N. T.)
104. All things work together for good to them that love God. (N. T.)
105. It is more blessed to give than to receive. (N. T.)
106. All they that take the sword; shall perish with the sword. (N. T.)
107. Go ye therefore and teach all nations. (N. T.)
108. Heaven and earth shall pass away, but my word shall not pass away. (N. T.)
109. Whoever shall exalt himself shall be abased, and he that shall humble himself shall be exalted. (N. T.)
110. What shall a man profit, if he shall gain the world and lose his own soul. (N. T.)
111. The tree is known by its fruit. (N. T.)
112. Therefore, all things whatsoever ye would that men should do to you, do ye even so to them. (N. T.)
113. Ask, and it shall be given to you; seek and ye shall find, knock and it shall be opened unto you. (N. T.)
114. Take no thought for your life, what ye shall eat or what ye shall drink. (N. T.)
115. When thou doest alms, let not thy left hand know what thy right hand doeth. (N. T.)
116. Ye are the light of the earth. A city that is set on a hill cannot be hid. (N. T.)
117. You pray in your distress and in your need. Would that you might pray also in the fullness of your joy and in your days of abundance. (Khalil Jebran)
118. You give but little when you give of your possessions. It is when you give of yourself that you truly give. (Khalil Jebran)
119. The lust for comfort, that stealthy thing that enters the home as guest, and then becomes a host, and then a master. (Khalil Jebran)
120. Thank God for sleep!
And when you cannot sleep
Still thank Him that you live
To lie awake. (Oxenham)
121. Everyone is his own doctor of divinity in the last record. (Stevenson)

122. Hammer away, ye hostile hands,
Your hammers break; God's anvil stands. (*Inscription on a memorial to the Huguenots in Paris*)
123. I sat down on a bumble bee
But I arose again,
And now I know the tenseness
Of humiliating pain. (*Crane*)
124. O money, money, money, I am not necessarily one of those who think thee holy.
But I often stop to wonder how thou canst go out so fast when thou comest in so slowly. (*Nash*)
125. Death sends a radiogram every day;
When I want you I'll drop in.
And then one day he comes with a
Master key and lets himself in and says,
"We'll go now." (*Sandburg*)
126. Laugh and the world laughs with you;
Weep and you weep alone.
For the sad old earth must borrow its mirth. (*Wilcox*)
127. God and the soldier,
All men adore
In time of trouble
And no more.
For when war is over
And all things righted,
God is neglected,
The old soldier slighted. (*Field*)
128. Libraries are not made, they grow. (*Birrell*)
129. Mother's arms are made of tenderness, and sweet sleep blesses the child who lies therein. (*Victor Hugo*)
130. People who know little are usually great talkers, while men who know much say little. (*Rousseau*)
131. What wisdom can you find that is greater than kindness? (*Linnaeus*)
132. I never trust my nose into other men's porridge. It is not bread and butter of mine. Every man for himself, and God for us all. (*Cervantes*)
133. I look upon all men as my compatriots. (*Socrates*)
134. Every tooth in a man's head is more valuable than a diamond. (*Cervantes*)
135. As Athenodorus was taking his leave of Caesar, "Remember,"

said he, "Caesar, whenever you are angry, to say or do nothing before you have repeated the four and twenty letters to yourself."

136. No good man ever grew rich all at once. (*Syrus*)
137. Patience is the best remedy for every trouble. (*Plantin*)
138. Consider the little mouse—how sagacious an animal it is which never entrusts life to one hole only. (*Planteus*)
139. No evil can happen to a great man, either in life or after death.
140. Whatsoever a man soweth, that shall he also reap. (*N. T.*)
141. He that plants thorns must never expect to gather roses. (*Bidpai*)
142. False words are not only evil in themselves, but they infect the soul with evil. (*Socrates*)
143. An Eastern philosopher used to say that there are only four kinds of people:
    1. Those who know not and know not that they know not. They are foolish.
    2. Those who know not and know that they know not. They are simple and should be instructed.
    3. Those who know and know not that they know. They are asleep and should be awakened.
    4. Those who know and know that they know. They are wise; follow them.
144. With malice towards none, with charity for all, with firmness in the right, as God gives us to see the right. (*Abraham Lincoln*)
145. Goodbye proud world; I'm going home;
    Thou art not my friend and I'm not thine. (*Emerson*)
146. Sir Humphrey Gilbert, on embarking on his ill-fated voyage homeward: "We are near to Heaven by sea as by land."
147. Gods fade, but God abides, and in man's heart,
    Speaks with the clear unconquerable cry
    Of energies and hopes that cannot die. (*Symonds*)
148. One man's wickedness may easily become all men's curse. (*Publius Syrus*)
149. Nothing can be more disgraceful than to be at war with him with whom you have lived on terms of friendship. (*Cicero*)
150. He removes the greatest ornament of friendship who takes away from it respect. (*Cicero*)
151. Do all the good you can
    By all the means you can
    In all the ways you can
    In all the places you can
    At all the times you can

        To all the people you can
        As long as ever you can. (*John Wesley's rule*)

152. While the sick man has life, there is hope.
153. Closed lips hurt no one; speaking may.
154. Xenophanes said, "I confess myself the greatest coward in the world, for I dare not do an ill thing."
155. What we gave we have,
What we spent we had,
What we left we lost.
156. In Fellowship Lies Friendship. (*Motto of the University Club of New York*)
157. Great is truth—fire cannot burn, nor water drown it. (*Alex. Dumas*)
158. Go tell the Spartans, thou that passeth by,
That here, abided to the law, we lie. (*Ceos*)
159. To everything there is a season, and a time to every purpose under the heaven. (*O. T.*)
160. There are seven secrets of child training mentioned by Maxwell:
    1. Watch your children with ceaseless vigilance.
    2. Maintain your God-appointed leadership.
    3. Help your children to find God for themselves as early as possible.
    4. Keep your children busy.
    5. Lay responsibilities upon your children and see they carry them out.
    6. Open the treasure house of new ideas.
    7. Make home the central attraction.
161. We have nothing to fear but fear itself. (*F. D. Roosevelt*)
162. Be not afraid of sudden fear, for the Lord shall be thy confidence. (*Proverbs 3:25, 26*)
163. After the verb "To love," "To Help" is the most beautiful verb in the world.
164. Thales was asked what was very difficult; he said, "To know one's self."
165. He that will not when he may,
When he will he shall have nay.
166. Handsome is that handsome does. (*Goldsmith*)
167. They are never alone that are accompanied with noble thoughts. (*Brooke*)
168. I see the beginning of my end. (*Massinger*)
169. The greater philosopher a man is, the more difficult it is for

him to answer the foolish questions of common people. (Shenkieweez)
170. Married in haste, we may repent at leisure. (Congreve)
171. An honest man's the noblest work of God. (Pope)
172. To die is a debt we must all of us discharge. (Euripides)
173. He who has not a good memory should never take upon him the trade of lying. (Montaigne)
174. Diogenes once saw a youth blushing, and said, "Courage, my boy, that is the complexion of virtue."
175. Cleanliness is indeed next to godliness. (Wesley)
176. All things change and we change with them.
177. Socrates said, "Bad men live that they may eat and drink, whereas good men eat and drink that they may live."
178. The God who gave us life gave us liberty at the same time. (Jefferson)
179. There is no such thing as death,
In nature nothing dies.
From each sad remnant of decay
Some forms of life arise.
180. Please, my heart, let the time for parting be sweet.
Let it not be a death, but completeness.
Let love melt into memory and pain into songs. (R. Tagore)
181. Make a rule, and pray to God to help you to keep it, never, if possible, to lie down at night without being able to say, "I have made one human being at least a little wiser, a little happier, or a little better this day." You will find it easier than you think, and pleasanter. (Kingsley)
182. Work is of a religious nature; work is of a brave nature; which it is the aim of all religion to be. All true work is sacred; in all true work, were it but true hand-labor, there is something of divineness. (T. Carlyle)
183. All human wisdom is summed up in two words—wait and hope. (Alex. Dumas)
184. Fear God. Honour the King. (N. T.)
185. Take heed that ye do not your alms before men, to be seen of them. (N. T.)
186. When thou doest alms, let not thy left hand know what thy right hand doeth. (N. T.)
187. Therefore all things whatsoever ye would that men should do to you, do you to them. (N. T.)
188. Be ye therefore wise as serpents, and harmless as doves. (N. T.)

189. Love thy neighbor as thyself. (N. T.)
190. It is easier for a rope to go through the eye of a needle, than for a rich man to enter into the Kingdom of God. (N. T.)
191. Inasmuch as ye have done it unto one of the least of these, my brethren, ye have done it unto me. (N. T.)
192. Physician, heal thyself. (N. T.)
193. Prove all things; hold fast that which is good. (N. T.)
194. A wise son maketh a glad father. (N. T.)
195. The memory of the just is blessed.
196. A good name is better than precious ointment.
197. All things work together for good to them that love God. (N. T.)
198. Unto the pure all things are pure. (N. T.)
199. Giving honour unto the wife, as unto the weaker vessel.
200. No man can serve two masters . . . ye cannot serve God and mammon. (N. T.)
201. Take no thought of your life, what ye shall eat or what ye shall drink. (N. T.)
202. By their fruits ye shall know them. (N. T.)
203. Judge not according to the appearance.
204. If God is with us, who can be against us?
205. God loveth a cheerful giver. (N. T.)
206. Out of the abundance of the heart the mouth speaketh. (N. T.)
207. Walk while ye have the light, lest darkness come upon you. (N. T.)
208. Greater love hath no man than this, that a man lay down his life for his friends. (N. T.)
209. It is more blessed to give than to receive. (N. T.)
210. I shall light a candle of understanding in thine heart which shall not be put out. (Apoc.)
211. Rejoice not over thy greatest enemy being dead, but remember that we die all.
212. Miss not the discourse of elders. (Apoc.)
213. Wine and women will make men of understanding to fall away. (Apoc.)
214. Whether it be to friend or foe, talk not of other men's lives. (Apoc.)
215. "Bury me on my face," said Diogenes. When asked why, he replied, "Because in a little while everything will be turned upside down."
216. A man asked Diogenes what was the proper time for supper, and

he made answer, "If you are a rich man, whenever you please; and if you are a poor man, whenever you can."
217. Diogenes was being asked whether it was better to marry or not. He replied, "Whichever you do, you will repent it."
218. Aristotle was asked which of those who tell lies gain by it. Said he, "That when he speak truth they are not believed."
219. Diogenes was once asked what a friend is, and his answer was, "One soul abiding in two bodies."
220. It takes a wise man to discover a wise man. (*Diogenes*)
221. Guard us from error in narration, and keep us from folly even in pleasantry, so that we may be safe from the censure of sarcastic tongues. (*Ben Ali Hariri*)
222. No one can harm the man who does himself no wrong. (*St. Chrysostom*)
223. Better be ignorant of a matter than half know it.
224. No good man ever grew rich all at once.
225. Diogenes, when a little before his death he fell into slumber, and his physician rousing him out of it asked him whether anything ailed him, wisely answered: "Nothing, sir; only one brother anticipates another." (*Sleep before death*.)
226. Cato requested old men not to add the disgrace of wickedness to old age, which was accompanied with many other evils.
227. When Philip had news brought him of divers and eminent success in one day, he said, "O Fortune, for all these so great kindnesses, do me some small mischief."
228. To be a good nurse one must be a good woman. What makes a good woman is the better or higher or holier nature: quietness, gentleness, patience, endurance, forbearance—forbearance with the patients, her fellow workers, her superiors, her equals. (*Quoted from Florence Nightingale's letter dated May 6, 1881*.)
229. Think that day lost whose descending sun views from thy hand no noble action done. (*Bobart*)
230. Julius Caesar wrote to his friend after he routed Pontius, "Veni, vidi, vici" (I came, I saw, I conquered).
231. Virtue is like precious odours—most fragrant when they are incensed or crushed. (*Bacon*)
232. Sometimes you see flies buried clearly in amber.
233. A sharp tongue is the only edged tool that grows keener with constant use. (*Irving*)
234. He who would write heroic poems should make his whole life a heroic poem. (*Carlyle*)

235. La carriere ouverte aux talens. (The tools to him that can handle them.) (*Napoleon*)
236. Whether we wake or we sleep,
Whether we carol or weep;
The sun with his planets in chime
Marketh the going of time. (*Fitzgerald*)
237. The disease of an evil conscience is beyond the practice of all the physicians of all the countries in the world. (*Gladstone*)
238. They who have steeped their souls in prayer,
Can every anguish calmly bear. (*Lord Houghton*)
239. The true pleasure of life is to live with your inferiors.
240. Do not pray for easy loves; pray to be stronger men!
Do not pray for tasks equal to your powers; pray for powers equal to your tasks. (*Brooks*)
241. Without haste, without rest!
Bind the motto to thy breast!
Bear it with thee as a spell;
Storm or sunshine, guard it well. (*Goethe*)
242. I would far rather be ignorant than wise in the foreboding of evil. (*Aeschylus*)
243. Gratitude is the sign of noble souls. (*Aesop*)
244. "George," said his father, "do you know who killed that beautiful little cherry tree yonder in the garden?" Looking at his father with the sweet face of youth brightened with the inexpressible charm of all-conquering truth, he gravely cried out, "I can't tell a lie, Pa; you know I can't tell a lie. I did cut it with my hatchet." (*The Life of George Washington*)
245. Now I lay me down to sleep,
I pray the Lord my soul to keep;
If I should die before I wake,
I pray the Lord my soul to take.
246. My God, my father and my friend,
Do not forsake me in my end. (*Dillon*)
247. Oh, the wasted hours of life
That have drifted by!
Oh the good that might have been
Lost without a sigh. (*Doodney*)
248. Carriages without horses shall go,
And accidents fill the world with woe.
249. Around the world thoughts shall fly
In the twinkling of an eye.

Under water men shall walk,
Shall ride, shall sleep and talk;
In the air men shall be seen—
In white, in black and in green.

Iron in the water shall float
As easy as a wooden boat. *Prophecy of Martha (Mother Shipton, 1488-1561)*

250. Sleep on, beloved sleep, and take thy rest;
Lay down thy head upon thy Saviour's breast.
We love thee well, but Jesus loves thee best—
Good night!

251. In the dark and trying days of the winter of 1939 when Great Britain stood alone against a formidable and ruthless foe, King George VI went to the microphone and delivered his Christmas message, as has been the custom of the royal house for many years. He ended his comforting message with this quotation from Louise Haskins:

> "I said to the man who stood at the gate of the year: 'Give me a light, that I may tread safely into the unknown'; and he replied, 'Go out into the darkness and put your hand into the hand of God. That shall be to you better than light and safer than a known way.'"

> To God the Father, God the Son
> And God the Spirit, Three in One,
> Be honor, praise and glory given
> By all on earth, and all in heaven.
>
> *(Doxology)*